SOCIAL JUSTICE, EQUALITY AND EMPOWERMENT

THE EQUAL PAY ACT, FIFTY YEARS ON

SOCIAL JUSTICE, EQUALITY AND EMPOWERMENT

Additional books in this series can be found on Nova's website under the Series tab.

Additional e-books in this series can be found on Nova's website under the e-book tab.

THE EQUAL PAY ACT, FIFTY YEARS ON

SUZANNA CROSS
EDITOR

nova publishers
New York

MT

Library of Congress Cataloging-in-Publication Data

ISBN: 978-1-63463-730-5

Published by Nova Science Publishers, Inc. † New York

4/26/16

CONTENTS

PREFACE

This book presents data trends in earnings for male and female workers and by discusses explanations that have been offered for the differences in earnings. It discusses the major laws directed at eliminating sex-based wage discrimination as well as relevant federal court cases.

Chapter 1 – Fifty years ago, President John F. Kennedy signed landmark legislation to guarantee equal pay for women and men performing equal work for the same employer. The Equal Pay Act of 1963 was the first in a series of major federal and state laws that had a profound effect on job opportunities and earnings for women over the next half century, and laid the foundation for the movement of women into the paid labor force at unprecedented levels. The following year, another groundbreaking law passed: the Civil Rights Act of 1964 prohibited discrimination on the basis of sex, race, color, national origin, and religion. Further cementing workplace protections between 1965 and 1967, President Lyndon B. Johnson issued a series of Executive Orders designed to ensure non-discrimination among Federal contractors. These critical legal advances bolstered five decades of economic and social progress for women – but much more remains to be done.

Chapter 2 – On May 10, 2013, President Obama signed a memorandum to the heads of executive departments and agencies on Advancing Pay Equality in the Federal Government and Learning from Successful Practices. This memorandum directed the Director of the U.S. Office of Personnel Management (OPM) to submit to the President a Governmentwide strategy to address any gender pay gap in the Federal workforce.

Chapter 3 – Report of U.S. Bureau of Labor Statistics, on Why do women still earn less than men?, dated June 2014.

Chapter 4 – The term "pay gap" refers to the difference in earnings between male and female workers. While the pay gap has narrowed since the 1960s, female workers with a strong attachment to the labor force earn about 77 to 81 cents for every dollar earned by similar male workers. Studies have analyzed the earnings and characteristics of male and female workers and found that a substantial portion of the pay gap is attributable to non-gender factors such as occupation and employment tenure. Some interpret these studies as evidence that discrimination, if present at all, is a minor factor in the pay gap and conclude that no policy changes are necessary. Conversely, advocates for further policy interventions note that some of the explanatory factors of the pay gap (such as occupation and hours worked) could be the result of discrimination and that no broadly accepted methodology is able to attribute the entirety of the pay gap to non-gender factors. The Equal Pay Act (EPA), which amends the Fair Labor Standards Act (FLSA), prohibits covered employers from paying lower wages to female employees than male employees for "equal work" on jobs requiring "equal skill, effort, and responsibility" and performed "under similar working conditions" at the same location. The FLSA exempts some jobs (e.g., hotel service workers) from EPA coverage, and the EPA makes exceptions for wage differentials based on merit or seniority systems, systems that measure earnings by "quality or quantity" of production, or "any factor other than sex." The "equal work" standard embodies a middle ground between demanding that two jobs either be exactly alike or that they merely be comparable. The test applied by the courts focuses on job similarity and whether, given all the circumstances, they require substantially the same skill, effort, and responsibility. The EPA may be enforced by the government, or individual complainants, in civil actions for wages unlawfully withheld and liquidated damages for willful violations. In addition, Title VII of the 1964 Civil Rights Act provides for the awarding of compensatory and punitive damages to victims of "intentional" wage discrimination, subject to caps on the employer's monetary liability. The issue of pay equity has attracted substantial attention in recent Congresses. A number of measures, including bills that would provide additional remedies, mandate "equal pay for equivalent jobs," or require studies on pay inequity, have been introduced in each of the last several congressional sessions. These bills include the Paycheck Fairness Act (H.R. 377/S. 84) and the Fair Pay Act (H.R. 438/S. 168) in the 113th Congress. This report also discusses pay equity litigation, including *Wal-Mart Stores v. Dukes*, a case in which the Supreme Court rejected class action status for current and former female Wal-Mart employees who allege that the company has engaged in pay discrimination.

In: The Equal Pay Act, Fifty Years on   ISBN: 978-1-63463-730-5
Editor: Suzanna Cross   © 2015 Nova Science Publishers, Inc.

Chapter 1

FIFTY YEARS AFTER THE EQUAL PAY ACT: ASSESSING THE PAST, TAKING STOCK OF THE FUTURE*

National Equal Pay Task Force

I. THE 50TH ANNIVERSARY OF THE EQUAL PAY ACT OF 1963

A. Foreword

Fifty years ago, President John F. Kennedy signed landmark legislation to guarantee equal pay for women and men performing equal work for the same employer. The Equal Pay Act of 1963 was the first in a series of major federal and state laws that had a profound effect on job opportunities and earnings for women over the next half century, and laid the foundation for the movement of women into the paid labor force at unprecedented levels. The following year, another groundbreaking law passed: the Civil Rights Act of 1964 prohibited discrimination on the basis of sex, race, color, national origin, and religion. Further cementing workplace protections between 1965 and 1967, President Lyndon B. Johnson issued a series of Executive Orders designed to ensure non-discrimination among Federal contractors. These critical legal advances

---

* This is an edited, reformatted and augmented version of a report issued June 2013.

bolstered five decades of economic and social progress for women – but much more remains to be done.

Since passage of the Equal Pay Act, several generations of women have transformed our workplaces and, in turn, our economy. Women have integrated many previously exclusively male job fields, and have achieved success at the highest levels of many fields. Women have achieved higher levels of education than ever before, and now serve at the highest levels of government, the judiciary, in Congress, and in private industry. They have become important sources of job creation, entrepreneurship, and innovation.

This progress notwithstanding, in 2011, the average woman still earned only 77 cents for every dollar earned by men.[1] Moreover, women continue to comprise a majority of employees in many low-wage sectors. For example, in 2012, fifty-two percent of all women in the full-time labor force worked in service, sales and office occupations, such as secretaries, cashiers, retail sales persons, maids, child care workers and customer service representatives, and comprised an overwhelming majority of the workers[2] in each of those sectors.

These sobering statistics matter. Women comprise nearly half of our workforce, and many women are the primary breadwinners for their families. Their level of earnings drive essential economic decisions – including decisions about quality of housing, access to medical treatment, educational attainment for children, child care, clothing, and food and other essentials. And of course, these earnings have a longterm effect on a woman's ability to save and prepare for retirement. When women are short-changed, their personal financial stability suffers, and their families suffer. But that is not all: women's lower earnings impact all levels and sectors of the economy, as well as local communities, since lower pay means fewer dollars are spent within neighborhood businesses or invested in new ventures. For these reasons, equal pay is important for our nation, the broader economic security of our families, and the growth of the middle class in our economy.

Fifty years ago, Congress and the President recognized that the Equal Pay Act was the first step to address overt sex-based compensation discrimination in employment that impeded women's ability to achieve workplace equality. The United States has made significant progress in widening the path to greater opportunities for women, but our work is not yet complete. With this report, we reaffirm our steadfast commitment to America and our national imperative of workplace equality for all.

The Task Force thanks the Council of Economic Advisors for their contributions to Part II of this report.

B. Introduction: The Evolution of Women's Economic Status between 1963 and 2013

The Equal Pay Act established a basic labor standard requiring employers to pay women and men the same wages when performing jobs that are equal, or substantially equal, in content. It was the first national labor standard to address a widespread practice of paying women less simply because they were women, and it laid the foundation for future workforce policies. Other important legislation and policies soon followed, which helped broaden employment opportunities for women and strengthened their ability to challenge unlawful discrimination.

Fifty years after passage of the Act, major shifts in the socio-economic status of women have transformed our nation's workplaces, communities, and families. This report explores the increase of women in the paid labor force since passage of the Equal Pay Act, and the passage of laws that have expanded civil rights protections for women experiencing unlawful pay discrimination. The first part of this report contains an assessment of workforce trends in three timeframes: 1960-1980; 1980-2000; and the early years of the 21st Century, from 2000-2010. Using data on labor force participation, earnings, occupations, educational attainment and entrepreneurship, and available data examining the differences among women by race/ethnicity and age, this report describes the progress of women in the paid labor force since the passage of the Equal Pay Act. It also compares women's status in the workforce to that of men and analyzes the evolution of women's and men's roles in the workplace, community, and family.

After reviewing five decades of data, the report addresses the status of equal pay for women today, the pay gap and other persistent challenges that remain in light of the fact that continued momentum has stalled in recent years. In the final section entitled, "2010 and Beyond," the report reflects on the efforts of President Barack Obama's Administration to eliminate the pay gap and on the federal equal pay agenda moving forward.

The Equal Pay Act and the Decades of Civil Rights Legal Advances That Followed

One year after passing the Equal Pay Act, Congress enacted the Civil Rights Act of 1964, a sweeping federal ban on discrimination. Title VII of the Act banned employment discrimination on the basis of race, color, religion, national origin, and sex. One year later, Executive Order 11246 prohibited federal government contractors from discriminating in employment and required them to engage in affirmative action to ensure equal opportunity based on race, color, religion, and national origin. Noticeably absent was any prohibition based on sex. In 1967, Executive Order 11246 was amended by Executive Order 11375, which prohibited discrimination on the basis of sex in hiring and employment within the federal government. Additionally, Title IX of the Education Amendments of 1972 opened the doors for women to pursue education free from discrimination in those educational institutions that received federal financial assistance. The Pregnancy Discrimination Act of 1978 strengthened employment discrimination protections for women who were pregnant, gave birth, or had related medical conditions. And in the 1990s, the Civil Rights Act of 1991 and the Family and Medical Leave Act of 1993 provided further protections for American workers, including broadening workplace leave rights for men and women and beginning to address critical barriers to full economic equality that stem from medical conditions and care giving responsibilities.

Economic and Social Progress, but a Persistent Pay Gap Remains

Women have made significant progress since the passage of the Equal Pay Act. Women's labor force participation rate in 2012 was 57.7 percent, over fifty percent higher than it was in the early 1960s.[3] In 1960, roughly 15 percent of managers were women; by 2009, almost 40 percent of managers were women.[4] The ratio of women's to men's annual earnings has narrowed from 59 cents for every dollar paid to men in 1963, to 77 cents in 2011.[5] The educational progress of women, who now outnumber men in their attainment of Bachelor's Degrees, Master's Degrees and Doctoral Degrees,[6] has driven the gains in earning power. Yet today, 50 years after the Equal Pay Act became law, a pay gap still exists, and studies have demonstrated that a significant portion of the wage gap cannot be fully explained when controlling for factors such as labor market experience and job characteristics.

The movement of women into the entrepreneurial ranks has offered women new earning opportunities. According to the Economic Census, in 1972, 486,009 firms were owned by women, but by 1982, the number had exploded to 2,612,621 firms. In 1982, receipts of women-owned firms reached $101,856,490, and they employed 1,254,588 employees and had payroll costs of $11,561,025.[7] More recently, the 2007 Census Survey of Business Owners reported that women's business ownership accounted for over a quarter of all businesses nationwide and generated over $1.2 trillion in business receipts.[8] That same year, the number of employees working in women-owned firms reached 7.6 million, with nearly half (45.9 percent) of all women-owned businesses operating in repair and maintenance industries; personal and laundry services; health care and social assistance; and professional, scientific and technical services.[9]

Occupational Segregation and Other Barriers to Equality Remain

Although working women have made progress in many areas, the workforce continues to be characterized by occupational segregation of women and men into different types of jobs. In Part II, this report discusses the potential impact of occupational segregation on the pay gap and some of the ways federal agencies intend to tackle that problem going forward.

In 1960, nearly two-thirds of working women were employed in clerical, service or sales positions. Thirteen percent of women held professional jobs, but even these posts were likely to be traditional women's jobs such as nursing or teaching positions.[10] Indeed, even the classified section in newspapers listed jobs separately for men and for women, a practice that would persist into the next decade. As women's educational attainment increased during the 1980s and beyond, so did women's movement into higher-paying professional and management jobs, where women now compose 51.5 percent of employed workers.[11] However, even today, women still are much more likely to enter occupations where the majority of workers are female, including the healthcare, education and human services fields. In addition, over half of all women continue to be employed in lower-paying sales, service and administrative support positions. Despite substantial gains in the management fields, women still lag behind in other non-traditional fields such as transportation, construction, and the science, technology, engineering and mathematics (STEM) fields.[12]

In addition to gender differences in occupations, there are differences based on race and ethnicity, as well as differences for women who are mothers. For example, White and Asian women are more likely to work in higher-paying management, professional and related occupations than Black and Hispanic women, who are more likely to work in lower-paying service occupations and significantly more likely to be among the working poor.[13] And mothers of children under 18 years of age in 2011 had lower median weekly earnings compared to other women.[14]

The Pay Gap Narrows, But Not Enough

Over the last 50 years, the wage gap between women and men has closed by 17 percentage points. Women earned on average 59.8 percent of men's pay in 1963, and today, the wage ratio is 77 percent.[15] The narrowing of the wage gap reflects in part larger economic changes affecting men and families. For instance, a change in the wage gap results not only from a raise in women's real earnings (those adjusted for inflation), but also from a drop in real earnings for men since the mid-1970s.[16] Women's real earnings have increased by about 71 percent from $21,646 in 1960 to $37,118 in 2011, while men's earnings have increased at a significantly lower rate, 35 percent, from $35,675 in 1960 to $48,202 in 2011.[17] Major shifts in our economy over the last fifty years, particularly in the move from a manufacturing base to services, information and communications technologies, have changed the skills and education workers need to compete successfully in a global market.[18] These changes have not been easy for some workers to navigate as new skills and education requirements have become more important. These economic shifts have contributed to the transformed role of women in our nation's families.[19] Today, the wages of women, both as single parents and as co-breadwinners, are critical to the overall economic health and stability of a majority of the nation's families.[20]

Even as women made inroads into non-traditional higher-paying occupations, pay for women compared to men across most occupational categories reflects a wage gap, regardless of the gender composition of detailed occupations. The higher-paying supervisory and management positions manifest many of the largest pay differences.[21] This persistent wage gap, even among higher-paying professions, is a longstanding problem. In 1983, twenty years after the law began to require equal pay for equal work, female managers and administrators earned just 64 percent of the pay of male workers in these jobs.[22] In addition, women – particularly Black women, who traditionally have had higher labor force participation rates and more experience in the labor market than women of other race/ethnic groups – experienced difficulty advancing into leadership positions.[23] This persistent barrier to career advancement into the top tiers of management drew the attention of the public and is known popularly as "the Glass Ceiling." Highly educated and skilled women of all races and ethnicities began reporting resistance and outright discrimination that prevented them from moving into the higher ranks of management. In 2011, some of the greatest differences in the median weekly earnings of women and men occurred in the category of management occupations.[24]

The Way Forward

The 50-year economic, social and political history described in the next section of this report sets the stage for the choices and challenges we face today. While the law recognizes the basic right to equal pay for substantially equal work and freedom from wage discrimination, women's earnings still fall short of men's. Although a generation of political organizing and cultural change has eliminated many barriers, women still face challenges entering the most highly-paid occupations. And although our country's prosperity depends on women at every level – from the family budget to the national economy – we still cannot say we fully and fairly value their contributions. With that reality in mind, in the final section of this report, we turn to the policy, enforcement, education and outreach work federal agencies are implementing – and the plan going forward – to ensure that equal pay becomes a reality. We ask Congress to do its part by passing the Paycheck Fairness Act, and we identify the major steps we must take to close the pay gap once and for all. A half century after President Kennedy made a national commitment to the cause of equal pay, our work remains unfinished. Today, we renew our commitment to the principle of equality for all of America's workers.

C. Five Decades of Equal Pay History

1960-1980: A Time of Social, Political and Economic Transformation for Women

An Overview of the Political Climate and Legislative Developments

On June 10, 1963, President Kennedy gathered a group of influential women in the Oval Office as he signed the historic Equal Pay Act into law. Attending the ceremony were women and men who had championed the legislation and made the case for its urgency.[25] In signing the bill, President Kennedy stated:

> The lower the family income, the higher the probability that the mother must work. Today, 1 out of 5 of these working mothers has children under 3. Two out of 5 have children of school age. Among the remainder, about 50 percent have husbands who earn less than $5,000 a year– – many of them much less. I believe they bear the heaviest burden of any group in our Nation. Where the mother is the sole support of the family, she often must face the hard choice of

either accepting public assistance or taking a position at a pay rate which averages less than two-thirds of the pay rate for men.[26]

While just over a third of all women were in the labor force in 1963,[27] the issue of pay discrimination was critically important to those working women and their families.

President Kennedy and advocates for the Equal Pay Act understood that the workforce was segregated greatly by gender and race. They also understood that, because the Act focuses on women and men working in the same occupations for the same employer, its reach would have limited benefits for the majority of women who did not work in jobs substantially the same as men's jobs. However, they saw the Act as an important first step.[28]

Despite its limitations, passage of the Equal Pay Act firmly supported women's economic rights and improved earnings. At the signing, President Kennedy explained that additional proposals to address the economic status of women were needed, and he fully expected his new Commission on the Status of Women, led by Eleanor Roosevelt and Assistant Labor Secretary Esther Peterson, to outline additional measures to boost the economic status of working women.

In October 1963, the Commission released *American Women: Report of the President's Commission on the Status of Women*. The report acknowledged the important, traditional roles of wife and mother. It also extensively documented the employment challenges women frequently faced when seeking employment and after becoming employed. These challenges included discriminatory practices that still resonate for women today – being denied employment and/or promotion, receiving unfair wages and fewer benefits, experiencing sexual harassment and workplace hostility, or facing discrimination on the basis of being pregnant.[29] These employment attitudes and actions impeded women's ability to obtain employment and advance in the workplace.

On the heels of the Commission's report, Congress passed and President Johnson signed the Civil Rights Act of 1964. In Title VII, the new law specifically addressed employment discrimination on the basis of race, color, religion, national origin, or sex. Sex was not originally among the prohibited bases of discrimination in the draft bill, but was inserted as an amendment during debate. When it passed with sex included, women gained a powerful new legal tool to fight workplace discrimination.[30]

An important factor in the tremendous changes in women's labor force participation, educational advancement, increased earnings and the role of mothers in the workforce over the last fifty years was the second wave of the U.S. women's movement. A growing political movement of women, including the leaders of traditional women's organizations, as well as new advocates who had been active in the civil rights movement, began visibly organizing. They recognized the need for a parallel political movement to challenge sex-based discrimination in a broad range of areas, including employment, housing, health care, access to credit, education, and child care.[31]

As increasing numbers of women became politically active and states formed their own commissions on the status of women, the call for more serious attention to discrimination against women grew louder.[32] In 1970, the Department of Labor issued sex discrimination guidelines interpreting Executive Order 11246 (prohibiting federal government contractors from discriminating in employment on the basis of race, color, religion, national origin and, because of the later amendment, sex) and addressed some of the more overt practices of discrimination and occupational segregation, such as advertising positions as "male help wanted" or "female help wanted."[33]

Equal pay rights expanded in 1972, with a series of key amendments to existing laws. Title IX of the Education Amendments of 1972, signed by President Richard M. Nixon, prohibited discrimination at educational institutions receiving federal funding. The prohibited discrimination included discrimination in rates of pay or any other form of compensation, and changes in compensation.[34] The 1972 Education Amendments also expanded the Equal Pay Act to cover executive, administrative, professional and outside sales employees.[35] In addition, in 1972, Congress strengthened Title VII by broadening its reach to public employers, educational institutions, and more private employers. As a result of these legislative changes, more women would have legal recourse for sex-based wage discrimination and other civil rights violations.

As the 1970s drew to a close, another significant piece of legislation for women — the Pregnancy Discrimination Act — was signed into law by President Jimmy Carter. This law amended Title VII of the Civil Rights Act to prohibit discrimination against pregnant workers, and to require that employers treat workers with pregnancy-related limitations the same way they treat other employees similar in their ability or inability to work.[36]

Increases in Women's Labor Force Participation and Educational Attainment

Against the backdrop of these laws that helped provide new employment and educational opportunities for women, and a growing socio-political movement, women began to enter the paid labor force in greater numbers and to seek higher levels of educational attainment. Women's labor force participation rate rose from 37.7 percent in 1960 to 43.3 percent in 1970, and to 51.5 percent by 1980.[37] The expansion of the overall female labor force largely reflected the influx of working mothers, whose labor force participation rates nearly doubled — from 27.6 percent in 1960 to 54.1 percent by 1980.[38]

Another noteworthy trend during this time was that, as the 1960s began, women's labor force participation rates varied greatly by race/ethnicity and marital and parental status. White women had a lower labor force participation rate than non-White women, but more specific data by race/ethnicity was not collected during this time.[39] Labor force statistics for Hispanic women were not collected by the Bureau of Labor Statistics until 1973; and, even then, the labor force participation rate for Hispanic women, hovering at 41 percent, was below that of Black and White women's participation rates, which were 49.8 and 44.1 percent, respectively. By 1980, the labor force participation rates of Black and White women were closer, at 53.1 and 51.2 percent respectively, while Hispanic women's labor force participation rate had climbed to 47.4 percent. Data for Asian women was not collected until 1990.[40]

For women with children, marital status also was a significant factor in labor force participation. When data on mothers by marital status first was collected in 1968, female single parents had a labor force participation rate of 61 percent, compared to 37 percent for married mothers. By 1980, female single parent participation rates had climbed to 68 percent while married mothers had increased their participation rates to 56 percent.[41]

Prior to 1980, the graphic representation of women's labor force participation rate by age resembled the letter "M," with a dip in women's participation during the prime child bearing and rearing years of ages 24-44. In contrast, men's graphic representation of labor force participation rates by age resembled an arc, and their participation reached its peak at ages 25-44. By 1980, the trend in greater labor force participation rates for women with children erased this graphical difference – so that the peak year of participation for women at ages 20-24 was followed by a slight decline by ages 25-34 and 35-54.

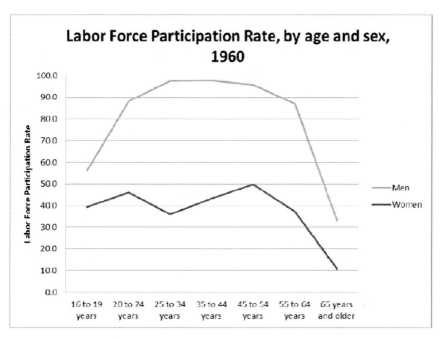

Source: Bureau of Labor Statistics, Current Population Survey. "Civilian labor force participation rates by age and sex, annual averages 1948-2012." (Unpublished table).

In addition to women's increased presence in the labor force, the 1960s-1980s witnessed a surge in the percentage of women obtaining Bachelor's, first professional and Master's Degrees. In 1960, only 35.3 percent of all Bachelor's Degrees were awarded to women, but by 1980, this figure had reached 49 percent. More dramatically, the proportion of first professional degrees awarded to women climbed from 3.6 percent in 1965 to 24.8 percent by 1980. Master's Degrees awarded to women climbed from 31.6 percent in 1960 to 49.2 by 1980.[42] The increase in women's educational attainment from 1960 to 1980 is one factor that contributed to a rise in earnings for women during the period. In contrast, real earnings for men increased greatly from 1960 and reached a peak in 1973, when they slowly began to fall through 1980.

Top Ten Nontraditional Occupations for Women in Rank Order by Number of Women, 1960 and 1980

Occupations	1960	1980
Farmers, managers, & tenant farmers	1	5
Farm laborers, wage workers	2	6
Accountants & auditors	3	
Janitors & sextons	4	2
Buyers and department heads, stores	5	
Stock clerks & storekeepers	6	
Salesmen & sales clerks, manufacturing	7	
Real estate agents & brokers	8	
Managers, food & dairy stores	9	
Postal clerks	10	
Nonfarm laborers -- stock handlers		3
Transport equipment operatives		1
Engineering & science technicians		4
Computer specialists		8
Protective service		7
Physicians, dentists, & related practitioners		9
Sales workers, except clerks, retail trade		10

Sources: Herman, A. M., & Castro, I. L. (1998). "Equal Pay: A Thirty-Five Year Perspective". Washington: U.S. Department of Labor. Page 19 - Table 2.

By 1980, thanks to advances in women's educational attainment, the number of women in STEM fields began to increase – even though women still comprised 25 percent or less of the total employed in STEM occupations.

By 1980, the most common non-traditional occupations for women included engineering and science technicians, computer specialists, physicians, dentists and related practitioners, as well as transport equipment operators, protective service and other positions on farms, handling stock or sales, or working as janitors.[43]

The change in the wage gap during this time period reflects the broader changes in women's labor participation and educational attainment. In 1960, the women's to men's earnings ratio stood at 60.7 percent, and it widened over time as men's real earnings climbed faster and more dramatically than women's, reaching its widest point – 56.6 percent – in 1973. But by 1980, the earnings ratio was nearly back to where it was in 1960 – 60.2 percent.[44]

Early Enforcement of the Equal Pay Act

During the 1960s and 1970s, the Wage and Hour Division of the Department of Labor enforced the Equal Pay Act. By 1965, the Department already had recovered a total of $156,202 under the Equal Pay Act on behalf of 960 employees. Only a year later, the number of workers found to be underpaid had risen dramatically to 6,633 – due a total of $2,097,600 under the Equal Pay Act. By 1969, the number of workers found to be underpaid under the Act nearly tripled to 16,100 workers due $4,585,344.[45] By the end of 1978, the Department of Labor had recovered $162,063,460 for over 269,601 workers.

During this twenty-year period – thanks to cases filed by government agencies and private plaintiffs – federal courts established some key interpretations of the Equal Pay Act. In 1969, Associate Solicitor of Labor Bessie Margolin argued the first appeal of an Equal Pay Act case, *Schultz* v. *Wheaton Glass Company*, and successfully convinced the United States Court of Appeals for the Third Circuit that the Equal Pay Act only required jobs to be "substantially equal," not identical.[46] The case involved female "selector-packers" who were paid less than male "selector-packer-stackers." In 1974, in *Corning Glass v. Brennan*, the Supreme Court held that a wage differential arising "simply because men would not work at the low rates paid women" was illegal under the Equal Pay Act.[47] In 1979, enforcement of the Equal Pay Act was transferred from the Department of Labor and the Civil Service Commission to the U.S. Equal Employment Opportunity Commission (EEOC).[48]

1980-2000: Women Advance in the Emerging Information Age

An Overview of the Social, Economic and Political Climate

The last two decades of the 20th Century were marked by significant growth in the educational attainment of women, a narrowing of the wage gap between women and men, and resistance to the occupational segregation and workplace barriers that limited advancement opportunities for working women. In 1980, the wage ratio between women and men stood at 60.2 percent. Over the next two decades, the wage gap narrowed noticeably – reaching 71.6 percent by 1990, and 73.7 percent by 2000.[49]

The 1980s began with a focused strategy among the leaders in women's organizations and unions to raise women's pay and to clarify the differences between the Equal Pay Act and Title VII of the Civil Rights Act's prohibition against sex-based wage discrimination. In 1981, the Supreme Court ruled, in *County of Washington v. Gunther*,[50] that Title VII was not limited by the equal work standard found in the Equal Pay Act. Strengthened by this decision, many state and local coalitions of unions, women's and civil rights organizations worked together to challenge the lower pay given to women who worked in traditionally female-dominated occupations where few men were employed.

Over 20 states, a number of local governments and some private sector firms began conducting job evaluation studies, and some made wage adjustments to ensure that men and women working in different types of occupations, but with similar job evaluation scores, were paid comparable wages.[51] Much of this action was achieved through union negotiation and state or local legislation. In addition to pay issues, working women frequently encountered outright sexual harassment and hostile workplaces. In 1980, the EEOC issued guidelines on sexual harassment, and the Supreme Court ultimately agreed in 1986 that Title VII's ban on sex discrimination in employment includes sexual harassment.[52] In 1991, Congress created the Glass Ceiling Commission to explore the challenges to women and people of color advancing in the labor force. In March 1995, the Commission issued *Good for Business: Making Full Use of the Nation's Human Capital,* a report documenting that women and minorities faced serious barriers to advancement to management and executive level positions. Further, where there were women and minorities in more senior positions, their compensation was lower than that of White males.[53]

In the 1990s, new federal laws ensured continued civil rights progress. Congress passed and President George H.W. Bush signed amendments to protect and expand Title VII following several Supreme Court decisions limiting its application. The Civil Rights Act of 1991 allowed Title VII plaintiffs, including those suing for intentional pay discrimination, to recover both compensatory and punitive damages subject to caps.

An additional barrier to the advancement of women in the workplace was lifted in 1993 when President William J. Clinton signed the Family and Medical Leave Act. This law provides eligible employees with up to 12 weeks of job-protected, unpaid leave for their own serious illness, that of their spouse, child or parent, and following the birth or adoption of a child. Employees are eligible for leave if they have worked for their employer at least 12 months, at least 1,250 hours over the past 12 months, and at a location where the company employs 50 or more employees within 75 miles.[54]

Soaring Educational Gains and Labor Force Participation Continue Through the End of the 20th Century

Women who were born in the wake of the Equal Pay Act, Title VII and Title IX of the Education Amendments Act came of age with a wide array of new educational and workforce opportunities. These young women achieved higher levels of education, while older women headed back to school, thus changing the male-to-female ratio at colleges across the United States. By 1981, women were earning half of all Bachelor's and Master's Degrees and over that decade gradually took the lead, earning 53 percent of all those degrees in 1990. This upward movement extended into the 1990s with women earning 57 percent of all Bachelor's Degrees and 58 percent of all Master's Degrees in 2000.[55] With regard to first professional degrees, women earned 25 percent of such degrees in 1980, 38 percent in 1990, and 45 percent by 2000. Among those seeking Doctoral Degrees, women earned 30 percent of such degrees in 1980, 36 percent in 1990, and 44 percent by 2000.[56]

Women who increased their educational attainment saw substantial gains in income but did not match the earnings of men with comparable education levels. By 1985, women with a Bachelor's Degree or higher witnessed their median weekly earnings match those of men holding just a high school diploma or equivalent. In 1992, these women's wages continued to climb until they bypassed the wages of men having received some college education or holding an associate's degree. These increases in wages continued through the remainder of the 1990s, but the wages of women with a Bachelor's Degree or higher remained lower than those of men with similar levels of education. Men with four years of college or more also saw real wage increases during this timeframe, so, in 2000, their earnings were approximately 35 percent higher than that of women with the same level of education.[57]

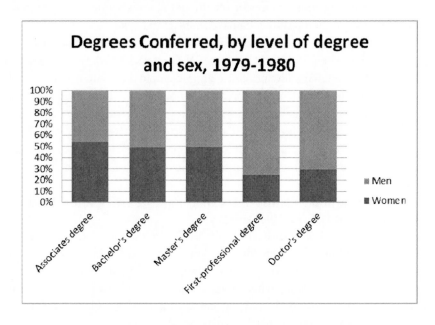

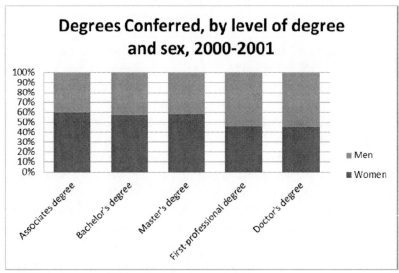

Source: Data from the National Center for Education Statistics, (2010) "Degrees Conferred by degree-granting institutions, by level of degree and sex of student: Selected years, 1869-70 through 2019-20."

The increased educational attainment of women contributed greatly to their overall increased earnings from 1980 to 2000 – with women's usual median weekly earnings growing by 23.4 percent over this time period.[58] However, most of the gains in earning power were reserved for women with a Bachelor's Degree or higher. The pay for these women increased by approximately 31 percent from 1980 to 2000. In comparison, women with less education saw much smaller or even no changes in earnings. Pay for women with some college rose by approximately 9 percent, while the real earnings of women with a high school diploma were virtually unchanged and decreased for women having less than a high school diploma.[59]

Women's Labor Force Participation Rates Continue to Increase; Married Women Maintain Participation Rates through Prime Child Bearing and Child Rearing Years

Over the last two decades of the 20th Century, women of all races continued to participate in the labor force in increasing numbers – with gains especially noticeable among married women with children. In 1980, White women's labor force participation rates were close to that of Black women at 51.2 and 53.1 percent, respectively, while Hispanic women's labor force participation rate had climbed to 47.4 percent. Between 1990 and 2000, Black women took the lead again in labor force participation – with 58.3 percent in 1990 and 63.1 percent in 2000, compared to White women, whose participation rate was 57.4 percent in 1990 and 59.5 percent in 2000. Hispanic women's labor force participation rate also grew from 53.1 percent in 1990 to 57.5 percent by 2000. When labor force participation data for Asian women first was collected in 1990, it showed the same labor force participation rates between White and Asian women in 1990 and 2000.[60] Even more significant was the increase in the labor force participation rate of married mothers with children, which climbed from 54.1 percent in 1980 to 66.3 percent in 1990 and 70.6 percent in 2000.[61]

For women with young children, marital status remained a significant factor in labor force participation. In 1980, mothers with children had similar labor force participation rates whether they were single (52 percent) or married (54.1 percent), while women who were divorced, widowed or separated had a higher labor force participation rate of 69.4 percent. By 2000, all mothers had increased their participation rate. For those who were divorced, widowed or separated, it reached 82.7 percent, while the rate for single mothers rose to 73.9 percent, and married mothers had a slightly lower participation rate of 70.6 percent.[62] The trend toward women remaining attached to the labor force through their prime child bearing and child rearing years continued during the latter half of the 20th Century and began to follow the pattern of men's labor force participation. In 1980 and 1990, women's labor force participation rate by age peaked at ages 25-34, similar to the years that men's labor force participation rate was highest. However, by 2000, the peak years for labor force participation had edged up to the 35-44 year age brackets for both women and men.[63]

Contribution of Married Women's Income to Family Income Grows
    The contribution of married women's earnings to overall family income also grew steadily during the latter half of the 20th Century – from just over a quarter of all family income (26.7 percent) in 1980 to one-third of family income (33.5 percent) in 2000.[64] In 1987, the Bureau of Labor Statistics began to collect data on the percentage of wives whose earnings were higher than their husband's, noting that, in 1987, 23.7 percent of wives earned more than their husbands, some of whom may not have worked at all. Among couples where both the husband and wife worked, 17.8 percent of wives earned the higher wages. This trend grew steadily throughout the 1990s, and by 2000, 29.9 percent of wives had higher earnings in families where the husband may not have been working. In families where both spouses worked, 23.3 percent of wives earned higher wages than their husbands.[65]

    Women's increased education and movement into higher-paying jobs may be one factor that accounts for the growth in families with higher-earning wives; however, another likely factor is the lack of increase in real earnings for men from 1980 to 2000. During this timeframe, women's real earnings rose by 23.4 percent on average, but men's earnings were essentially unchanged.[66] In its September 1997 report, *Money Income in the United States: 1996*, the U.S. Census Bureau noted that the narrowing of the wage gap was not necessarily cause for celebration. "Recent increases in the female-to-male earnings ratio have been due more to declines in the earnings of men than to increases in the earnings of women," it said.[67] By 2000, earnings for both men and women had started to rise slowly again; however, the wage gap held steady at 73.7 percent.[68]

Wage Gap Narrows Significantly in the 1980s, but Progress Slows during the 1990s
    The last two decades of the 20th Century were marked by significant growth in the educational attainment of women, as well as a significant narrowing of the wage gap between women and men as women enjoyed the

returns on their higher investments in education and accumulated labor-market experience. In 1980, the ratio between women's and men's earnings stood at 60.2 percent. Over these two decades, the wage gap narrowed considerably – the wage ratio reached 71.6 percent by 1990, and 73.7 percent by 2000.[69]

In 1998, the President's Council of Economic Advisors (CEA) issued a report which found that, although the pay gap had narrowed substantially between the signing of the Equal Pay Act in 1963 and 1998, "there still exists a significant wage gap that cannot be explained by differences between male and female workers in labor market experience and in the characteristics of jobs they hold." The report cited a detailed longitudinal study in the 1980s that found about one-third of the gender pay gap was explained by differences in the skills and experience that women bring to the labor market, and another 28 percent was due to differences in industry, occupation and union status among men and women. Roughly 40 percent of the pay gap could not be explained. The CEA concluded that "one indirect and rough measure of the extent of discrimination remaining in the labor market is the 'unexplained' difference in pay."[70]

Enforcement Actions

In the 1980s and 1990s, the EEOC enforcement activities included significant work on behalf of working women seeking equal opportunity and equal pay. In 1980, the EEOC held hearings on sex-based job segregation and wage discrimination; and, commissioned by the EEOC, the National Academy of Sciences published a report in 1981 entitled, *Women, Work and Wages: Equal Pay for Jobs of Equal Value.*

In 1984, General Motors Corporation (GM) and the United Auto Workers agreed to pay $42.4 million to resolve an EEOC Commissioner charge alleging the company engaged in a "pattern and practice" of race and sex discrimination. The settlement also provided that GM would promote a substantial number of minorities and women into managerial jobs, as well as recruit minorities and women into high-paying apprenticeship and craft programs. At that time, the settlement was the largest non-litigated settlement in the history of the EEOC.

One significant compensation case, *EEOC v. Allstate Insurance*, resulted in a 1985 consent decree between the EEOC and Allstate, resolving an Equal Pay Act claim that the company paid a lower guaranteed minimum salary to females than to males performing the identical job of sales agent. Under this decree, $5 million was distributed to approximately 3,200 women. In the same year, the Commission successfully settled a sex discrimination suit against

Teachers Insurance and Annuity Equity Fund. This suit resulted in recalculating pension benefits in a "sex neutral manner" for over 800,000 female workers.

In 1986, the EEOC published its Interpretations of the Equal Pay Act, replacing those issued by the U.S. Department of Labor.

In 1995, the EEOC held a series of meetings devoted to hearing the views of experts and advocates on the effectiveness of the EEOC in its enforcement of laws prohibiting discrimination in employment. In his opening statement, EEOC Chairman Gilbert F. Casellas observed that "[t]he Commission has been criticized for paying insufficient attention to wage disparity" and stated that "[o]ur summons, with the help of the organizations present today, is to better use the tools provided by our existing authority to force employers who perpetuate wage-based inequities to examine their motivations and rectify the wrongs." In 1994, 9,600 charges of wage discrimination were filed with the Commission under the Equal Pay Act, Title VII of the Civil Rights Act, Title I of the Americans with Disabilities Act, and the Age Discrimination in Employment Act. Most of the charges were brought under Title VII, and the lion's share of the Title VII cases were based on race and/or gender.

In 1997, the EEOC issued an Enforcement Guidance on Sex Discrimination in the Compensation of Sports Coaches in Educational Institutions.[71] The Commission issued this guidance because, although Congress had outlawed sex-discrimination in school-sponsored athletics programs over twenty-five years prior (with the passage of Title IX), then-recent studies showed that the overall pattern of the employment and compensation of coaches by educational institutions was still far from gender-neutral. The Commission wanted to assist both coaches and educational institutions in better understanding their rights and responsibilities.

Military Conflict	Number of Women Served
Spanish-America War	1,500
WW1	10,000+
WW2	40,000
Korean War	120,000
Vietnam Era	7,000
Persian Gulf War	41,000
OEF / OIF	200,000+

Source: U.S. Department of Veterans Affairs. America's Women Veterans: Military Service History and VA Benefit Utilization Services (2011),http://www.va.gov /vetdata/docs/SpecialReports/Final_Womens_Report_3_2_12_v_7.pdf

2000-2010: Progress Stalls, Enforcement Efforts Redoubled

An Overview of the Economic Climate

The 21st Century unfolded with great hope and expectations. As technology transformed our basic means of communication and revolutionized our workplaces, it carried a promise for easing the work-life challenge experienced by the majority of working families, opening more opportunities for women in the growing technology sector and continued progress in closing the wage gap between women and men.[72] Yet, despite these hopes, the early years of the 21st Century are notable for stalled progress and dips in labor force participation, particularly among working mothers of young children.

A volatile first decade of the 21st Century brought the worst economic crisis since the Great Depression, which greatly changed the economic conditions of our nation and increased the economic pressure felt by families all across the country. The heightened need for security and build-up of military units also brought with it more opportunities for women to serve in the ultimate non-traditional jobs – military occupational specialties in the U.S. armed forces. The number of women in the military has varied greatly over the years, but reached a high of over 200,000 women during the Operation Enduring Freedom and Operation Iraqi Freedom (OEF/OIF) conflicts.[73]

While women's contributions to family income rose in importance in the lead-up to 2000, the new century's economic challenges illustrated that women's earnings often proved crucial to families' financial survival.

Increased Educational Attainment and its Effect on Earnings

The new century began with women holding solid majorities in the attainment of Bachelor's, Master's and Doctoral Degrees, earning 57 percent of all Bachelor's Degrees and 58.5 percent of all Master's Degrees in 2000. These numbers held steady for Bachelor's Degrees through 2009 but increased slightly for post-graduate degrees, with women awarded 60.4 percent of all Master's Degrees, 49 percent of all first professional degrees, and 52.3 percent of Doctoral Degrees by the end of the decade.[74]

Education continued to be an important factor in increasing women's earnings throughout the first part of the 21st Century, but the earnings gains were not shared equally by women of different races/ethnicities. In 2011, among women of all race/ethnic groups with Bachelor's Degrees, Asian women had the highest median weekly earnings, at $946. White women followed with median weekly earnings of $939, while Hispanic women and

Black women had significantly lower median weekly earnings – $862 and $843, respectively.[75]

From 2000 to 2010, real median earnings for full-time, year-round male workers remained mostly unchanged, while women's earnings edged up by 3.4 percent early in the decade, then held steady through 2011.[76] Educational attainment was an important factor in earnings, even though a wage gap between educated women and men persisted. College-educated workers saw the highest financial returns to their education. Meanwhile, men without advanced education saw earnings drop, and women with lower educational attainment saw little movement in wages.[77] These trends influenced the slight change in the female-to-male wage ratio, which rose from 73.7 percent to 76.3 percent between 2000 and 2001. The wage ratio has hovered near this point throughout the remainder of the 2000s – hitting a high of 77.8 percent in 2007, only to retreat to 77 percent in 2011.[78]

Changes in Labor Force Participation Rates

Between 2000 and 2010, labor force participation rates declined slightly for all women, but most dramatically for Black women, going from a high of 63.1 percent in 2000 to 59.9 percent by 2010. Black women still maintained higher labor force participation rates than other women, who saw only slight declines in their participation rates. In 2010, White women's labor force participation rate was 58.5 percent, Hispanic women's rate stood at 56.5 percent, and Asian women were at 57.0 percent.[79] During this time period, the labor force participation rates of men also dropped, reflecting the impact of the recession, as well as an increase in the number of older workers retiring from the labor force.

The labor force participation rate of married mothers, with spouse present, also declined during this period, dropping from 70.6 percent in 2000[80] to 69.7 percent in 2010.[81] For women with young children, being married was associated with a lower labor force participation rate. In 2010, mothers with children under age 6 who were married, with spouse present, had a labor force participation rate of 62.5 percent, while mothers with all other marital statuses had a rate of 68.2 percent.[82] The drop in married mothers' labor force participation rate, particularly the rate for those with young children, led to considerable public discussion about the difficulties that professional women with children faced in the workforce.

The older workers' role in the economy also took on greater significance during the early 2000s. Women's labor force participation rates by age continued to follow the trends for men through the early part of the 21st

Century, with both men and women having the highest labor force participation rates later in life – in the 45-54 year-old age bracket. This shift in the ages of peak labor force participation, with a higher participation rate among the 45-54 year olds, is markedly different from the previous fifty years and is one reflection of the greater presence of older workers in the labor force as the U.S. population ages.[83]

Contribution of Married Women's Income to Family Income

The contribution of married women's earnings to overall family income continued to grow steadily throughout the first decade of the 21st Century, going from 33.5 percent in 2000 to 37.6 percent by 2010.[84] The percentage of wives with higher incomes than their husbands grew even more dramatically. In 2000, 29.9 percent of wives earned more than their husbands, some of whom may not have worked at all, and by 2010, this figure had reached 38.8 percent. Among couples where both the husband and wife worked, 23.3 percent of wives had higher earnings than their husbands in 2000, while 29.2 percent of wives were the higher earner by 2010.[85]

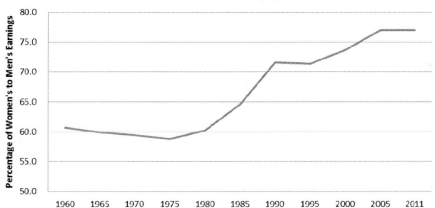

Women's Median Annual Earnings as a Percentage of Men's

Source: U.S. Census Bureau. (2011). "Women's Earnings as a Percentage of Men's Earnings by Race and Hispanic Origin." *Historical Income Tables.* http://www.census.gov/hhes/www/income/data/historical/people/.

Enforcement Actions

From fiscal year 2000 to 2009, the EEOC found reasonable cause to believe discrimination had occurred in 829 charges of pay discrimination under all of the statutes it enforces, and recovered over $52.7 million for charging parties in those cases through administrative enforcement.[86] The EEOC also litigated a significant number of sex-based wage discrimination cases throughout this decade, including the 2004 case *EEOC v. Morgan Stanley & Co.*, in which the EEOC obtained $54 million for sex-based discrimination in compensation, promotion, and other aspects of employment.

With more women serving as the primary or co-breadwinner in families, concern increased about long working hours and the conflict experienced by women and men who were both in the workforce and responsible for caring for young children, elderly parents or disabled family members.[87] The EEOC sought to address this issue in 2007 with enforcement guidance on unlawful disparate treatment of workers with caregiving responsibilities.[88]

In 2007, the Supreme Court issued its ruling in *Ledbetter v. Goodyear Tire & Rubber Co.*,[89] igniting controversy when it struck down the longstanding interpretation of Title VII's timeliness rules held by the EEOC and many courts. The case began in March 1998, when Lilly Ledbetter, who was employed at the Gadsden, Alabama, plant of Goodyear Tire and Rubber Company, filed a charge with the EEOC alleging that she had received a discriminatorily low salary as an area manager because of her sex in violation of Title VII of the Civil Rights Act. Ledbetter only discovered how much her male co-workers were making when someone left an anonymous note in her mailbox showing her pay and that of the three males who were doing the same job. In an interview, she stated that she worked for a company that told her, "You do not discuss wages with anyone in this factory."[90] The court ruled that, because the later effects of past discrimination did not restart the clock for filing an EEOC charge, Ledbetter's claim was untimely. The outcome was at odds with the longstanding interpretation of wage discrimination timeliness rules held by the EEOC and many courts, and highlighted the significant problem of pay secrecy.

The Ledbetter case helped raise the visibility of the equal pay issue and generated a major organizing campaign to reverse the decision in Congress. In response, Congress passed and President Obama signed the Lilly Ledbetter Fair Pay Act of 2009, effectively restoring the previous timelines for filing Title VII charges of pay discrimination with the EEOC. Further, President Obama addressed the ongoing challenge of equal pay and the persistent wage gap between women and men by creating the National Equal Pay Task Force in January 2010.[91]

During this decade, OFCCP continued to address pay discrimination through its enforcement activity under Executive Order 11246. In 2002, a $4.1 million settlement with Coca Cola for pay discrimination on the basis of race and sex benefitted over 900 current and former female employees at the company's Atlanta, Georgia, headquarters, many of whom held professional positions. In 2004, OFCCP resolved another large systemic pay discrimination case combining the issues of pay and sex discrimination in a $5.5 million settlement with Charlotte, North Carolina-based Wachovia Corporation. In that case, OFCCP alleged that more than 2,000 female workers had been underpaid.

II. 2010 AND BEYOND: WORKING TO CLOSE THE GAP

We have witnessed five decades of economic progress for women, supported by the expansion of civil rights and sweeping changes in the role of women in the workplace and our national economy. Yet women still face a significant gender gap in pay, one that seems to be closing far more slowly than in earlier decades, despite significant gains in education and workforce participation.

There are multiple ways to measure the pay gap – but under all of them, and with or without considering occupation, female and minority workers earn significantly less than White male workers. According to the latest Bureau of Labor Statistics data, women's weekly median earnings are about 81 percent of men's.[92] And looking at annual earnings reveals even larger gaps – approximately 23 cents less on the dollar for women compared with men.[93] The wage gap also is greater for women of color: Black women earn approximately 70 cents and Hispanic women make approximately 60 cents for every dollar earned by a non-Hispanic White man, according to Bureau of Labor Statistics data; and 64 cents for Black women and 56 cents for Hispanic women, according to Census data. Minority men face a wage gap as well when compared to White men – about 21 cents for Black men and about 29 cents for Hispanic men based on weekly wage data.[94] Ultimately, no matter how you look at the data, a persistent pay gap remains. Decades of research shows a gender gap in pay even after factors such as the type of work performed and qualifications (education and experience) are taken into account. These studies consistently conclude that discrimination likely explains at least some of the remaining difference.[95]

Fifty years later, we still have much work to do. We can continue to improve existing federal enforcement efforts through better strategic collaboration, and improve data collection and investigative tools. We can pass the Paycheck Fairness Act, so the Equal Pay Act will better safeguard the right to equal pay for equal work. Finally, we can expand our vision of equal opportunity. We can take on the array of practices and preconceptions – such as occupational segregation – that contribute to inequality for working women (and some men). We can break down the remaining barriers that prevent us from achieving true equality in the workplace.

Closing the pay gap is not just a moral imperative; it would confer broad economic and social benefits on our nation, its workers, and their families. Ensuring that workers who are underpaid due to discrimination can earn a fair wage means they can better support themselves and their families, thereby lifting countless children out of poverty. It also will help grow the middle class. Over the longterm, equal pay will provide a broader economic base for our nation – one that benefits all workers and their families.

A. 50 Years Later – Not Equal, Not Yet

Today, the U.S. workforce is rich in diversity of gender, race and age. Overall, 58.1 percent of U.S. women were in the labor force in 2011, with Black women continuing to lead at 59.1 percent and White women close behind at 58 percent. Asian women's participation in the labor force stood at 56.8, and Hispanic women had the lowest rate at 55.9 percent.[96] Working mothers continue to represent a significant number of working women, and their labor force participation rates were highest for single mothers at 74.9 percent, while married women had a rate of 69.1 percent. A majority of older women, 59.5 percent of those aged 54 to 65, were present in the workforce. These figures are just slightly lower than the historic labor force participation rates that were achieved in 1999, and show that a majority of women remain strongly attached to paid employment.[97]

Women continue to lead in educational attainment, earning more Bachelor's, Master's and Doctoral Degrees than men and nearly half of all professional degrees. Women's choice of college major also holds promise for greater gains in non-traditional occupations. Recent female college graduates are now earning nearly half of all the degrees in natural resources and conservation, homeland security and law enforcement, half of all business administration degrees, and more than half of all degrees in biological sciences and the health professions.[98]

And in the field of entrepreneurship, women's growing presence represents a total economic impact of nearly $3 trillion to the U.S. economy. In 2008, women entrepreneurs produced employment for over 23 million workers – especially significant considering that only 20 percent of women-owned firms had employees.

Despite these gains, the workforce continues to be segregated by race and gender – particularly when it comes to occupation. This occupational segregation has important implications for closing the pay gap, because women are segregated into low-paying occupations and also typically earn less than men in the same field. Addressing the barriers that prevent women from having equal access to higher-paying occupations and ensuring fair pay within occupations are critical strategies for closing the pay gap.

In addition to gender differences in occupations, there are differences based on race and ethnicity. For example, White and Asian women are more likely to work in higher-paying management, professional and related occupations than Black and Hispanic women, who are more likely to work in lower-paying service occupations and significantly more likely to be among the working poor.[99]

Occupational segregation has decreased since the mid-20th Century but is far from elimination.[100] Forty- four percent of employed men work in occupations that are over three-quarters male, while only 6 percent of working women are in these same occupations.[101] As recently as 2010, nine of the ten most common occupations for women were majority female – administrative assistants, nurses, cashiers, retail salespersons, nursing and home health aides, waitresses, retail sales supervisors and managers, customer service representatives, and house cleaners.[102] Examples of fields that remain at least 75 percent male include manufacturing salespersons, farmers and ranchers, architects, transportation supervisors, cutting workers, detectives and investigators, and computer programmers.[103]

Occupational segregation has persisted despite the many other economic and social transformations described in Part I of this report. Indeed, the top 10 occupations held by women did not vary much between 1960 and 1980. Nursing aides, orderlies and attendants appeared among the top 10 list for the first time in 1975, but remained among top jobs for women until 2000.[104] In 2010, the list looked little different than in 1980 – with variation in the leading occupations often due to changes in definitions and occupational groupings over time.

Ten Leading Occupations of Women in Rank Order by Numbers of Women, 1960, 1980, 2000 and 2010

Occupations	1960	1980	2000	2010
Private household workers	1	8	---	
Secretaries*(1)	2	1	1	
Retail trade, sales clerks*(2)	3	3		
Elementary school teachers*(3)	4	7	4	
Bookkeepers*(4)	5	2		
Waiters and waitresses	6	5		7
Nurses, professional (Registered Nurses)	7	6	6	2
Sewers and stichers, manufacturing	8	---		
Typists	9	9	---	
Cashiers	10	4	8	4
Nursing aides, orderlies, & attendants*(5)	---	10	7	
Retail & personal sales workers, including cashiers*(2)			2	
Managers & administrators, n.e.c.			3	
Sales supervisors & proprietors			5	
Bookkeepers, accounting, & auditing clerks*(4)			9	
Accountants & auditors			10	
Secretaries & administrative assistants* (1)				1
Elementary & middle school teachers *(3)				3
Cashiers				4
Retail salespersons *(2)				5
Nursing, psychiatric, and home health aides *(5)				6
First-line supervisors/managers of retail sales workers				8
Customer service representatives				9
Maids & housekeeping cleaners				10

Sources: Census Bureau. U.S. Census Population: 1960, Vol. 1; Statistical Abstract of the United States: 1963; and U.S. Bureau of Labor Statistics, Labor Force Statistics Derived from the Current Population Survey: A Databook, Vol. 1 (1982), and U.S. Department of Labor Women's Bureau, "Leading Occupations for Women in 2000", and "20 Leading Occupations of Employed Women, 2010 Annual Averages" (based on BLS Current Population Survey data).

Notes: *() notes a change in the name and or occupational grouping with a number that corresponds to a closely related occupation

In 1960, among non-traditional occupations for women – those in which women constituted 25 percent or less of those employed – women mostly held jobs on farms, in offices and retail establishments, or as clerks and sales positions for manufacturers, real estate or postal offices. Over the next twenty years, many of these occupations began to employ even greater numbers of women, so they no longer were male-dominated occupations. For instance, buyers in department stores, real estate agents, sales representatives and clerks in manufacturing facilities, managers in food and dairy stores, accountants and auditors and postal clerks all moved off the list of jobs that were non-traditional for women. Indeed, the decline in occupational segregation between 1970 and 2009 was largely a result of women moving into traditionally-male, white-collar occupations;[105] as a result, heavily male jobs have become increasingly blue-collar.

In recent decades, two areas that historically were almost exclusively male – the STEM fields and the military – have begun to open to women. By 1980, thanks to advances in women's educational attainment, the number of women in STEM fields began to increase – even though women still comprised 25 percent or less of the total employed in the STEM occupations. Notably, women who hold STEM degrees and work in STEM occupations earn 33 percent more, on average, than women in non-STEM jobs; and, while women in non-STEM occupations typically earn 23 percent less than their male colleagues, the salaries of their counterparts in STEM fields are only 14 percent less than those of their male co-workers.[106]

Women's service in the active duty armed forces steadily increased, especially after 2000. A total of 41,000 women served in the military during the Persian Gulf War.[107] By the end of November 2012, the number of women in the military reached 204,973. Of that total, 38,378 women were officers, and 164,021 women were enlisted.[108]

In recent years, changes in both law and policy have altered women's roles and the military jobs they are allowed to perform. Throughout U.S. military history, various rules and regulations have limited women's official involvement, rank attainment, and role within the services. However, according to the Pentagon, women frequently found themselves in combat during the wars in Iraq and Afghanistan. Hundreds of thousands of women have deployed in those conflicts and, unlike in previous wars, performed numerous functions that effectively put them directly in harm's way.[109] In January 2013, then-Secretary Leon Panetta recognized the exceptional service of women in the Iraq and Afghanistan wars by moving to open more military positions – including positions in ground combat – to women.

While occupational segregation is sometimes described as a simple matter of women's choices, historical patterns of exclusion and discrimination paint a more complex picture. Two general frameworks can explain occupational segregation: one based on workers and one based on employers. On the employer side, occupational segregation may be due to discrimination that can take several forms, including outright refusal to hire, severe harassment of women in non-traditional jobs, or policies and practices that screen qualified women out of positions but are not job-related.[110] An alternative framework emphasizes worker differences. For example, one group may be more willing to accept unpleasant or dangerous work, longer hours, or physical strain in return for higher wages. As another example, women may enter occupations that require less investment and result in less earnings growth because they expect abbreviated and discontinuous labor force activity.[111]

These two frameworks are not incompatible: the interaction between labor market discrimination and societal discrimination may have indirect effects that reinforce gender differences. For example, labor market discrimination can affect women's economic status indirectly by reducing their incentives to invest in themselves and to acquire particular job qualifications.[112]

For example, women are significantly underrepresented in STEM fields. According to statistics available from the National Center for Education Statistics, in 1970, fewer than 10 percent of new Bachelor's Degree graduates in business, computer science, engineering and newly graduating doctors and lawyers were women. By 2010, women were equally likely to graduate in business, law, and medicine as men.

However, less than one-third of new computer science graduates, and an even smaller fraction of new engineers, were women. A survey of undergraduate women at the University of Minnesota found that female undergraduates expressed lack of interest, had expectations of not being welcome in the profession, as well as exaggerated impressions of difficulty of the coursework in these fields.[113] Another study found that women were more likely to leave engineering compared to other fields because of dissatisfaction over pay and promotion opportunities.[114]

Regardless of the underlying causes, occupational segregation fuels the wage gap because average wages in "female" occupations are lower, even holding constant other observable characteristics such as education. This pattern is illustrated in Table 1, which highlights the most segregated occupations for each type of degree required. As the table shows, average wages in typically "female" occupations are significantly lower for each degree requirement category.

Table 1. Average Wages for Male and Female Dominated Professions

Male Dominated Professions Requiring a High School Diploma	Percent Male	Average Wage	Female Dominated Professions Requiring a High School Diploma	Percent Female	Average Wage
Brickmasons, blockmasons, and stonemasons	99.9	$ 45,410	Secretaries and administrative assistants	95.3	$ 34,660
Tool and die makers	99.2	$ 39,910	Childcare workers	94.1	$ 19,300
Pipelayers, plumbers, pipefitters, and steamfitters	98.7	$ 46,660	Hairdressers, hairstylists, and cosmetologists	92.8	$ 22,500
Carpenters	98.4	$ 39,530	Receptionists and information clerks	91.5	$ 25,240
Electricians	98.2	$ 48,250	Tellers	87.3	$ 24,100
Average		**$ 43,952**	**Average**		**$ 25,160**
Male Dominated Professions Requiring a Bachelor's Degree or Higher	Percent Male	Average Wage	Female Dominated Professions Requiring a Bachelor's Degree or Higher	Percent Female	Average Wage
Mechanical engineers	95.5	$ 78,160	Speech-language Pathologists	95.2	$ 66,920
Computer control programmers and operators	91.6	$ 71,380	Occupational Therapists	94	$ 72,320
Aerospace engineers	91	$ 97,480	Dietitians and nutritionists	93.3	$ 53,250
Electrical and electronics engineers	91	$ 87,180	Librarians	86.8	$ 54,500
Chiroprators	88.7	$ 67,200	Special education teachers	86.2	$ 53,220
Average		**$ 80,280**	**Average**		**$ 60,042**

Note: Occupations grouped by entry-level education requirement reported in the BLS Occupational Outlook Handbook. Source: Bureau of Labor Statistics, Current Population Survey, Occupational Outlook Handbook.

To see the extent to which occupational segregation affects average wages, we plot the relationship between the average wage in the occupation—relative to what would be expected given the age and education level of the workers in the occupation—and the share of females in the occupation.[115] Figure 1 shows these results. Each observation corresponds to an occupation. There is a distinct negative relationship between average wage in the occupation and female share, with every 10 percentage point increase in female share associated with a 4 percent decline in average wages. In other words, women in female-dominated occupations seem to earn less than we would otherwise expect based on their age and education. And while we do not know the extent to which this phenomenon is explained by historical patterns of exclusion and present-day discrimination, or by worker decisions, or by a combination of the two, decreasing the degree of occupational segregation could have a significant impact on closing the wage gap.

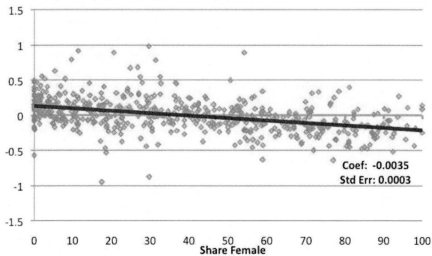

Note: The vertical axis corresponds to the occupation average wages that would be
      expected given the age and education level of workers.
Source: March Current Population Survey, 2010-2012.

Figure 1. Occupation Specific Wage and Female Share.

In addition to the effects of occupational segregation, research findings and Bureau of Labor Statistics data show women regularly are paid less than men working in the same occupation and in some cases even the same job. Controlling for differences in the types of jobs women and men typically perform, women earn less than men in male-dominated occupations (such as managers, software developers, and CEOs) and in female-dominated occupations (such as teachers, nurses, and receptionists).[116] The pay gap exists for women with advanced degrees, corporate positions, and high-paying and high-skill jobs, just as it does for low- and middle-income workers. For example, in a recent study of newly trained doctors, even after controlling for the effects of specialty, practice setting, work hours and other factors, the gender pay gap was nearly $17,000 in 2008.[117]

A widely debated contention about the pay gap is that it is attributable to women's choices to put family ahead of work. However, the gender pay gap exists for women working full time as well as part time, and begins when women are first employed, which is often well before they have children.[118] Regardless of whether work hours could explain some portion of the wage gap, research shows there is a "motherhood penalty" for female workers with children, stemming from stereotypes and biases about working mothers. Researchers have found the mere fact of parenthood for women leads to perceptions of lowered competence and commitment, and lower salary offers.[119] The same research shows, however, that men are not penalized for having children and in some ways benefit.

To the extent discrimination limits the opportunities for women to enter more highly paid occupations, we need strategies designed to open these doors. To the extent that equal pay for equal work remains elusive, we must redouble our efforts. Understanding the impact of family responsibilities on the pay gap and ensuring that women are not penalized for their status as mothers is another important part of closing the gap over the long term. The next section sheds light on those strategies – including enforcement, education, training, and more tools for workers to know their worth and how to act on it.

B. Closing the Gap – The Way Forward

On January 27, 2010, during his State of the Union address, President Obama pledged "to crack down on violations of equal pay laws – so that women get equal pay for an equal day's work."[120] To carry out that pledge to strengthen federal equal pay enforcement, the White House simultaneously announced the creation of a National Equal Pay Task Force composed of the major federal agencies that enforce our nation's pay discrimination laws. The Task Force brings together the expertise and resources of four federal agencies: the Equal Employment Opportunity Commission (EEOC), the Department of Justice (DOJ), the Department of Labor (DOL), and the Office of Personnel Management (OPM). Collectively, these agencies have jurisdiction over several key federal employment laws that protect our nation's public and private sector workers.[121] Both the achievements of the Task Force and its member agencies and its agenda for the coming years help frame a national strategy to close the pay gap once and for all.

As the White House announcement explained:

> The President is establishing a National Equal Pay Task Force. To make sure we uphold our nation's core commitment to equality of opportunity, the Obama Administration is implementing an Equal Pay initiative to improve compliance, public education, and enforcement of equal pay laws. The Task Force will ensure that the agencies with responsibility for equal pay enforcement are coordinating efforts and limiting potential gaps in enforcement. The Administration also continues to support the Paycheck Fairness Act, and is increasing funding for the agencies enforcing equal pay laws and other key civil rights statutes.[122]

The Task Force approach also reflected the larger goal of developing a unified civil rights agenda in the federal government. Just as intelligence agencies must share information to protect our national security, so too must civil rights agencies work together to safeguard the rights and economic security of all workers.

C. Achievements of the National Equal Pay Task Force

Shortly after the Task Force's creation, members developed a set of recommendations and goals to structure its collaboration on compliance, public education, and enforcement.[123] Those recommendations addressed five identified "persistent challenges" to the effective enforcement of equal pay laws, providing a road map for the work of the Task Force member agencies over the coming years:

1) Interagency Coordination. Different federal agencies have different federal responsibilities for equal pay enforcement under different laws, and lack of coordination leaves gaps in enforcement. The Task Force proposed to close those gaps and maximize the impact of existing enforcement tools through strengthened interagency coordination.

2) Available Data Sources. Existing available data sources on the private workforce are inadequate. The Task Force recommended improvements in data collection on the private workforce to better understand the pay gap and better apply limited enforcement resources.

3) Outreach and Public Education. Both employees and employers lack information about the wage gap and their legal rights and responsibilities. In response, the Task Force planned extensive outreach and public education materials for employers and employees, as well as training programs for the investigators at their member agencies.

4) Pay Gap in Federal Workforce. An eleven-cent wage gap for the federal workforce shows the need to address these issues for public employees. The Task Force directed the EEOC and OPM to develop a plan to identify the sources of this gap and address them.

5) Passage of the Paycheck Fairness Act. Current laws addressing unequal pay could be strengthened through additional legislation. The Task Force supported passage of the Paycheck Fairness Act to address loopholes in current law.

In June 2011, OFCCP settled a lawsuit against multi-national pharmaceutical corporation AstraZeneca, involving claims the company paid certain female sales associates less than their male counterparts. Under the terms of the settlement, AstraZeneca agreed to pay $250,000 to 124 female employees who worked at the company's business center in Wayne, Pennsylvania. AstraZeneca also agreed to re-examine its pay practices in offices across 13 states and the District of Columbia, to determine if women in that position were being underpaid and to adjust salaries accordingly.

In July 2010, Vice President Biden publicly released the Task Force recommendations.[124] Since then, Task Force member agencies have been building the infrastructure for an unprecedented level of collaboration across the federal government. By putting aside old turf battles and seeking opportunities to reduce duplication and maximize efficiency, Task Force members have been working to ensure that all workers get fair pay.

D. 2011 – 2013: Establishing the Infrastructure for Improved Equal Pay Enforcement

The early years of the Equal Pay Task Force's work largely consisted of developing the infrastructure for improved enforcement of equal pay laws, including achieving a number of specific milestones related to implementing the first recommendation of improved interagency coordination. This infrastructure development rested on two pillars: the development of mechanisms for interagency collaboration to enhance federal law enforcement agencies' capacity to identify and remedy illegal pay discrimination, and efforts to ensure federal regulations and policy provided the strongest possible framework for the enforcement of equal pay laws.

The development of mechanisms for improved interagency collaboration on equal pay laws also fostered a more integrated federal approach to civil rights enforcement broadly. Under the leadership of EEOC Chair Jacqueline Berrien, Assistant Attorney General for Civil Rights Tom Perez and OFCCP Director Patricia Shiu, agencies reinvigorated existing Memoranda of Understanding to facilitate information sharing, conducted pilot projects aimed at improving interagency collaboration in enforcement, built interagency relationships, facilitated joint outreach efforts, and trained together to ensure a shared understanding of civil rights laws and of each agency's role in enforcing them.

In November 2011, the EEOC and OFCCP issued a revised Memorandum of Understanding (MOU) aimed at strengthening collaboration between the two agencies. The revised MOU promotes effective collaboration in the agencies' enforcement efforts, reduces duplication, and maximizes efficiency. The EEOC and OFCCP conducted a pilot project in 2011 and 2012, focused on improving collaboration in enforcement, facilitating joint outreach, and maximizing efficiencies through joint training and cross training. Drawing on the improved information sharing provisions in the revised MOU, the EEOC and OFCCP worked collaboratively on dozens of investigations and audits, conducted dozens of joint outreach events, and trained together on areas of shared jurisdiction, such as compensation discrimination. The collaboration conserved valuable tax dollars by avoiding duplicative effort, and helped lay the groundwork for interagency collaboration on more complex issues in the future.

The EEOC and DOJ also worked to improve interagency collaboration in the enforcement of federal civil rights laws, including equal pay laws. Through a pilot project involving the EEOC's Philadelphia, Chicago, Los Angeles and

San Francisco District Offices, the EEOC and DOJ worked to improve collaboration early in EEOC's investigations of charges of discrimination against state and local government employers, thereby reducing the need for time-consuming and duplicative supplemental investigations. Since 2010, the EEOC and DOJ have collaborated on over 220 charges, on issues including pay discrimination and sex segregation in assignment. To date, lawsuits filed as a result of the project have included one involving sex-segregated job assignments at a correctional facility in Ohio and one involving the termination of an employee after she announced her pregnancy. Additionally, since the Task Force began, the EEOC and DOJ worked together to bring a joint enforcement action against the Texas Department of Agriculture in which the agencies obtained monetary relief under the Equal Pay Act and Title VII for three women who were paid less than their male counterparts.

> Tabatha Wagner learned that she was paid less than a male colleague who was hired after her at Hyundai Ideal Electric Company. After she raised the issue, she was fired in retaliation for complaining. The EEOC sued, and in May 2011, Hyundai Ideal Electric agreed to pay $188,000 to Ms. Wagner to settle the lawsuit. As part of the settlement, the company also agreed to provide training for all human resource personnel and employees at their Mansfield, Ohio facility, to help prevent future violation of federal employment discrimination laws.

In addition to developing the infrastructure to support a robust interagency approach to equal pay enforcement, Task Force agencies spent considerable resources developing the strongest possible regulatory and policy framework to support it. One of the most notable achievements in this area was the rescission of two 2006 guidance documents known as the "Compensation Standards" and "Voluntary Guidelines" that created arbitrary barriers to OFCCP enforcement of pay discrimination in violation of Executive Order 11246. In addition to rescinding the old guidance documents, OFCCP provided new guidance for contractors and other interested stakeholders setting forth the procedures, analysis and protocols OFCCP will utilize going forward. These new procedures align OFCCP enforcement with Title VII principles, and with the approach of its sister agencies on the Task Force, the EEOC and DOJ.[125]

Since 2010, the Task Force also has been working to implement the second recommendation on improved data collection. In August 2010, the EEOC commissioned a study by the National Academy of Sciences to determine the type of pay data the EEOC should collect to enhance wage discrimination law enforcement, and how best to collect that data.[126] The National Academy of Sciences issued its report in August 2012, calling on the EEOC, DOJ and OFCCP to develop a comprehensive plan for the use of compensation data, and providing analysis of how compensation data may be used in enforcement efforts.[127] In August 2011, OFCCP issued an Advance Notice of Proposed Rulemaking (ANPRM) soliciting stakeholder input on the design and use of a potential compensation data collection tool.[128] The EEOC, OFCCP and DOJ are working in close coordination to develop integrated, complementary plans for pay data collection.

Task Force member agencies also have made progress on the third recommendation, better education and outreach for employees and employers. In collaboration with other National Equal Pay Act Task Force members, both the EEOC and the Women's Bureau initiated education and outreach events in cities across the nation to educate women about their rights and employers about their responsibilities. The Bureau released two new publications, *A Woman's Guide to Equal Pay Rights* and *An Employer's Guide to Equal Pay*, and an Equal Pay Toolkit, which can be found on the agency's website.[129] Led by the Women's Bureau, the Department of Labor, in conjunction with the Equal Pay Task Force, issued an "Equal Pay App Challenge." This challenge invited developers to use publicly available data and resources to create applications that accomplish at least one of the following goals: provide greater access to pay data broken down by gender, race, and ethnicity; provide interactive tools for early career coaching; help inform negotiations; or promote online mentoring. The winning apps, which help empower and educate users, were announced at a ceremony at the Department of Labor during the summer of 2012.[130]

All agencies also are collaborating on outreach and on training within their agencies, which saves resources and ensures a consistent federal strategy on equal pay. Some highlights include:

- The Department of Labor's Women's Bureau, in partnership with the Department's Office of Public Engagement and Center for Faith-Based Neighborhood Partnerships, convened a series of briefings to highlight the plight of America's most vulnerable workers. The series, named "Vulnerable Women Workers," assembled national women's organizations, private foundations and government agencies to learn more about the working conditions and gender-based pay equity challenges of vulnerable workers.

- In 2011, the EEOC hosted twenty-eight Equal Pay Day events around the country with participation from Task Force agency members, experts in equal pay advocacy, and private sector leaders. Over 2,000 people attended the various events, in cities such as Atlanta, Birmingham, Boston, New York, Phoenix, Miami, Nashville, Cheyenne, Los Angeles, and Salt Lake City.

- A 2012 Equal Pay Tweet Up, hosted by the Department of Labor with participants from the EEOC, DOJ and community leaders, was a nationally trending topic and generated substantial discussion and visibility around equal pay efforts.

- In 2013, the Women's Bureau co-led eighteen Equal Pay Day events around the country with participation from Task Force agency members, experts in equal pay advocacy, and private sector leaders. Over 1,100 people attended the various events, in cities such as Atlanta, Kansas City, Boston, Dallas, Denver, San Francisco, Seattle, Philadelphia, and Chicago.

- Also in 2013, in collaboration with the Department of Labor's OFCCP and Office of the Chief Economist, the Women's Bureau hosted an equal pay web chat. Experts from each of the agencies were on hand to discuss wage inequality and ongoing policy initiatives, and directed participants to resources designed to help workers. More than 350 people participated in the chat and received immediate responses to their many questions.

- Finally, the Women's Bureau maintains a webpage dedicated to providing the public with the most current tools, resources and information on equal pay. The page, found at http://www.dol.gov/equalpay/, includes the latest translations of guides for women and employers on equal pay rights and obligations, links to the facts sheets on women's earnings developed by the Women's Bureau and the Bureau of Labor Statistics, and OFCCP's Equal Pay Enforcement statistics.

Lorelei Kilker is an analytical chemist for an environmental laboratory. She lives in Brighton, Colorado with her domestic partner and their two children.

In October 2011, Ms. Kilker was one of a class of women who benefitted from the EEOC's investigation of alleged systematic sex discrimination at her former employer. The EEOC found that Western Sugar denied women training and promotions, gave them less desirable work assignments and segregated positions by gender, denied year-round employment, and paid lower wages to women at its Ft. Morgan, Colorado facility.

The EEOC obtained back wages and significant remedial relief through conciliation with the employer.

The Task Force also is working to ensure the federal government is a model employer when it comes to ensuring equal pay for all workers, addressing the fourth recommendation outlined above. The EEOC and OPM continue to work closely on equal pay, building on the commitment made by EEOC Chair Jacqueline Berrien and then-OPM Director John Berry in their July 2011 joint memorandum to federal employees pledging their commitment to the vigorous enforcement of pay discrimination laws as they apply to federal employees. Task Force members, led by OPM, have developed a number of programs aimed at improving women's participation at the highest levels of federal service, including the development of an online portal for Federal Women Program Managers and programs on Work-Life Effectiveness.

In order to further understand how the practices of executive departments and agencies (agencies) affect the compensation of similarly situated men and women, and to promote gender pay equality in the federal government and more broadly, President Obama issued a May 10, 2013 Presidential Memorandum, titled "Advancing Pay Equality in the Federal Government and Learning from Successful Practices." The Presidential Memorandum directs OPM to submit a government-wide strategy to address any gender pay gap in the federal workforce. Each agency is required to review pay and promotion policies and practices to facilitate development of the strategy.

During this time, each agency also has substantially increased its effectiveness in the enforcement of pay discrimination laws, as a result of all of these specific improvements in collaboration, coordination, policy, outreach, training, and individual agency initiatives.

- From the Task Force's formation in January 2010 through March 31, 2013, the EEOC obtained over $78 million in relief for victims of sex-based wage discrimination through administrative enforcement.

- OFCCP similarly has recovered more than $33 million in back wages and nearly 7,000 job opportunities on behalf of over 60,000 victims of discrimination. During this period, OFCCP reviewed the pay practices of over 14,000 businesses that employ over 5.6 million workers – and closed more than 80 compliance evaluations with financial settlements remedying pay discrimination on the basis of gender and race. Through those efforts, OFCCP recovered a total of $2.5 million in back pay and salary adjustments for more than 1,200 workers who were victims of pay discrimination. In 2011, OFCCP more than doubled the number of compensation cases closed with financial remedies over the number closed in 2010 – and successfully resolved an even greater number of compensation cases in 2012.
- DOJ concentrated on opening opportunities for women in the higher paying law enforcement jobs and entered into settlements with police departments, correctional facilities, and other public employers where women are underrepresented in non-traditional positions.[131]

E. 2013 and Beyond: The Way Forward

As we mark the 50th Anniversary of the Equal Pay Act in 2013, the Task Force has achieved a number of the milestones that it set for itself in 2010 and is continuing to move forward, working toward passage of the Paycheck Fairness Act and addressing the broad array of issues that contribute to inequality for working women.

In 2013, Task Force agencies are moving from exploring collaboration and developing collaboration tools to making interagency collaboration a regular component of their agencies' enforcement work. This effort includes regular tri-agency meetings with the leadership of the EEOC, OFCCP and Department of Justice Civil Rights Division, active implementation of the revitalized MOU to ensure regular information-sharing between the EEOC and OFCCP at the headquarters level and among the agencies' field offices, and the application of the lessons of the interagency pilot projects to make specific improvements in enforcement procedures.

In addition, Task Force agencies are focusing on how better data can improve enforcement. One of the biggest obstacles to combating pay discrimination is that so many women do not know they are being underpaid due to discrimination and many employers prohibit the sharing of pay data. To address the implications of pay secrecy norms and policies, the Task Force continues to focus on the importance of pay data collection. The EEOC, OFCCP and DOJ continue to work closely together as they consider the use of pay data in enforcement efforts.

Better enforcement of existing civil rights laws will help, but those laws also leave gaps that must be filled. Congress, too, has an important role to play, by passing the Paycheck Fairness Act. This Act would address the current loopholes in existing law; strengthen remedies for pay discrimination; increase outreach and education to working women; provide technical assistance to small businesses; ensure that employees can discuss their wages without risk of being fired; and provide additional research and resources to fight pay inequity.

Finally, even with better enforcement and better laws, we also need an equal pay agenda that addresses the broad array of issues that contribute to wage inequality. We must continue to enforce the nation's laws prohibiting employers from paying women and men differently for the same work. And we also must address pay discrimination within a broader framework of practices that may limit the full economic participation of women workers.

Addressing Occupational Segregation

For example, we must break down discriminatory barriers that exclude women from traditionally male-dominated occupations, which pay more than traditionally female dominated occupations. In its work on sex discrimination issues, the DOJ has focused on cases that open non-traditional positions – such as police and correctional officer jobs – to women, and OFCCP has renewed its focus on increasing opportunities for women in the construction industry. OFCCP's new pay discrimination guidance also is intended to broaden the agency's focus on practices such as channeling and glass ceilings that wrongly exclude women from higher paying job opportunities. The EEOC always has been a leader in addressing systemic discrimination against women in employment through administrative enforcement and litigation efforts, and will continue to be a leader in this realm in the future. In sum, the agencies are working to ensure that these jobs – solid middle- class jobs that allow workers to provide for their families' futures – are not closed to women workers on the basis of sex.

> For a number of years Amanda McMillan of Jackson, Mississippi worked as a secretary for the owner of a Forrest City Grocery Company. She was doing many of the same duties as male salespeople, but at lower pay.

> Despite repeatedly asking for a promotion to the better and higher-paying job in sales, she was told by the company that the job of a salesman was too dangerous for a woman, and that she would not be a good mother if she were on the road meeting customers.
>
> The EEOC sued Forrest City for sex discrimination on McMillan's behalf, and obtained $125,000 in monetary damages and an agreement to provide ongoing training for management on sex discrimination.
>
> When asked why she has pursued the case, McMillan said, "I'm doing this because it was wrong and I could never look my girls in the face and then tell them they live in America and could be anything they wanted to be."

In addition to improved enforcement, we can educate and empower workers to take better advantage of these open doors. One example is the focus that the Council on Women and Girls and White House Office of Science and Technology have placed on increasing the participation of women and girls, as well as other underrepresented groups, in the fields of science, technology, engineering, and mathematics. Strategies include increasing the engagement of girls with STEM subjects in formal and informal environments, encouraging mentoring to support women throughout their academic and professional experiences, and supporting efforts to retain women in the STEM workforce. Another example is providing workers better information, mentoring and negotiation tools, through apps such as those developed by the Department of Labor's app challenge.

Addressing the Overlay of Discrimination Based on Race, Ethnicity and Gender in Compensation

The pay gap for women of color compared with White men is bigger than the gap for all women compared with men. Task Force agencies enforce laws that challenge illegal pay discrimination whether it is based on race, national origin, disability, or gender, or a combination of factors. Understanding and addressing how the pay gap impacts women (and men) of color will be another important focus in 2013 and beyond.

Addressing Discrimination against Mothers and Caregivers

Addressing the wage gap for women also includes addressing the problem of discrimination based on stereotypes about the proper role of women and mothers. Pregnancy and caregiver discrimination continue to limit the employment opportunities of women, and require enforcement and public education to equal employment opportunity in our nation's workplaces.

III. CONCLUSION: CLOSING THE GAP – WHAT'S AT STAKE

Closing the pay gap is the right thing to do – but it is also an economic necessity. Closing the gap could have broad benefits for reducing poverty, growing the middle class and boosting our nation's economic growth. Economists widely agree that reducing inequality is a net economic positive – both in terms of the ability of individual workers to get better jobs at better pay, and in terms of the overall beneficial effect on our economy.

Discrimination imposes real costs on our economy – preventing our nation from fully enjoying the talents of all its workers, and unfairly limiting the employment and wage prospects for entire classes of people. In recent decades, increases in U.S. economic inequality have fallen disproportionately on women and minorities. For example, the declining value of the minimum wage has had a significant negative effect on women – who head one quarter of households with children.

Ultimately, the differences in pay for women and men compound over the years. According to an analysis by the Department of Labor's Chief Economist, by age 25, the average young woman working full time would have already earned $5,000 less over the course of her working career than the average 25-year old man. If that earnings gap is not corrected, by age 65, she will have lost hundreds of thousands of dollars over her working lifetime.[132] Fewer dollars for workers and their families means a real loss of economic security, at a time when no family can afford to be earning less.

Since the 1960s, women have moved into the paid labor force in record numbers. The share of women participating in the paid labor force has increased from 37.7 percent in 1960 to 57.7 percent in 2012. By 2012, female earners contributed to family income in 65 percent of the families with at least one wage earner. Among families with children, the share is even larger at 70 percent. Given the rising importance of women's earnings in family income, closing the pay gap is important to improving family outcomes, such as reducing the number of individuals, and especially children, who live in poverty. What would happen to poverty rates if women's hourly wages were increased by 10 percent, an increase that still would not fully close the pay gap? In 2011, approximately 46.2 million individuals – including nearly 16 million children – were living in poverty. Raising all working women's wages by 10 percent would lift nearly 1.3 million individuals out of poverty, including more than half a million children.[133]

Reducing occupational segregation also is likely to benefit not only individual workers and their families, but the economy as a whole. Reducing inequality means that individual workers facing illegal barriers to good middle-class jobs or a fair paycheck will see personal gains in employment and wages. Improving the economic prospects of millions of American workers and their families will increase demand and boost job creation overall. Indeed, a recent paper by Hsieh, Hurst, Jones and Klenow (2013) finds that 15 to 20 percent of aggregate wage growth between 1960 and 2008 was due to a decline in barriers to occupational choice.[134] Employers also stand to benefit from a more equal society, as workers can be better matched to jobs and workplaces increase access to the diverse talent we need to help our companies compete in a 21st Century global economy.

Hard work should lead to a decent living for all Americans. Workers should know their worth and be empowered to claim it. Federal agencies should safeguard the right to equal pay and make certain all employers play by the same rules. Employers should share best practices for providing equal opportunity in the workplace. It should not take another fifty years to close the wage gap.

In marking Equal Pay Day this year, the President said, "[w]age inequality undermines the promise of fairness and opportunity upon which our country was founded." Fifty years after the Equal Pay Act's passage, we have taken important steps toward fulfilling that promise, but our journey is not complete. As we pause to honor this anniversary, we recommit ourselves to closing the gap – once and for all.

End Notes

[1] U.S. Census Bureau. "Women's Earnings as a Percentage of Men's Earnings by Race and Hispanic Origin." *Historical Income Tables, Table P-40.* (2011). http://www.census.gov /hhes/www/income

[2] Bureau of Labor Statistics, U.S. Department of Labor. "Employed persons by occupation, sex and age." *Current Population Survey.* (2013). http://www.bls.gov/cps/cpsaat09.htm.

[3] Bureau of Labor Statistics, U.S. Department of Labor. "Employment status of the civilian noninstitutional population by age, sex, and race." *Current Population Survey.* (2012). http://bls.gov/cps/cpsaat03.htm; Bureau of Labor Statistics, U.S. Department of Labor.

"Labor Force Participation: 75 Years of Change, 1950-98, and 1998- 2025." (1999).
http://www.bls.gov/mlr/1999/12/art1full.pdf.

[4] U.S. Census Bureau. "Percentage of Managers who are women: 1940-2009." *Women in the Labor Force*. (2010). http://www.census.gov/newsroom/pdf/women workforce slides.pdf.

[5] U.S. Census Bureau. "Women's Earnings as a Percentage of Men's Earnings by Race and Hispanic Origin." *Historical Income Tables, Table P-40*. (2011). http://www.census.gov /hhes/www/income

[6] National Center for Education Statistics, U.S. Department of Education. "Bachelor's, master's, and doctor's degrees conferred by degree-granting institutions, by sex of student and discipline division: 2010-2011." *Digest of Education Statistics*. http://nces.ed.gov/programs /digest/d12/tables/dt12 317.asp.

[7] Herman, A. M., & Castro, I. L. U.S. Department of Labor. "Equal Pay: A Thirty-Five Year Perspective." 62, Table 7. (1998).

[8] U.S. Census Bureau. "Census Bureau Reports Women-Owned Firms Numbered 7.8 Million in 2007, Generated Receipts of $1.2 Trillion." *Newsroom*. (2010). http://www.census.gov /newsroom/releases/archives/businessownership/cb10-184.html.

[9] U.S. Census Bureau. "Census Bureau Reports Women-Owned Firms Numbered 7.8 Million in 2007, Generated Receipts of $1.2 Trillion." *Newsroom*. (2010). http://www.census.gov /newsroom/releases/archives/business ownership/cb10-184.html.

[10] Herman, A. M., & Castro, I. L. U.S. Department of Labor. "Equal Pay: A Thirty-Five Year Perspective." 17. (1998).

[11] Bureau of Labor Statistics, U.S. Department of Labor. "Employed persons by detailed occupation and sex, 2012 annual averages." *Current Population Survey*. (2013). http://www.bls.gov/cps/cpsaat11.htm.

[12] Bureau of Labor Statistics, U.S. Department of Labor. "Women in the Labor Force: A Databook, 2012." *BLS Reports*. (2013). http://www.bls.gov/cps/wlf-databook-2012.pdf.

[13] Bureau of Labor Statistics, U.S. Department of Labor. "Women in the Labor Force: A Databook, 2012." *BLS Reports*. (2013). http://www.bls.gov/cps/wlf-databook-2012.pdf.

[14] Bureau of Labor Statistics, U.S. Department of Labor. "Median usual weekly earnings of full-time wage and salary workers, by sex, marital status, and presence and age of own children under 18 years old, 2011 annual averages." *Highlights of Women's Earnings in 2011*. 45. (2012) http://www.bls.gov/cps/cpswom2011.pdf.

[15] U.S. Census Bureau. "Income, Poverty, and Health Insurance Coverage in the United States: 2011," 48, Table A4. (2012). http://www.census.gov/prod/2012pubs/p60-243.pdf.

[16] U.S. Census Bureau. "Income, Poverty, and Health Insurance Coverage in the United States: 2008." 36. (2009). http://www.census.gov/prod/2009pubs/p60-236.pdf.

[17] U.S. Census Bureau. "Full-time, year-round workers by median earnings and sex: 1960 to 2011." *Historical Income Tables*. http://www.census.gov/hhes/www/income

[18] Lacey, T.A and Wright, B. "Employment Outlook: 2008-18, Occupational employment projections to 2018." *Monthly Labor Review, November 2009*. 82-123. (2008). www.bls.gov/opub/mlr/2009/11/art5full.pdf.

[19] Levitan, S.A & Belous, R.S. "Working wives and mothers: What happens to family life?" *Monthly Labor Review, September 1981*. 26-30. (1981). www.bls.gov/opub/mlr/1981/09 /art4full.pdf.

[20] Bureau of Labor Statistics, U.S. Department of Labor. "Employment Characteristics of Families—2011." *BLS Reports*. (2012). http://www.bls.gov/news.release/famee.nr0.htm.

[21] Bureau of Labor Statistics, U.S. Department of Labor. "Median usual weekly earnings of full-time wage and salary workers, by detailed occupation and sex, 2011 annual averages."

Highlights of Women's Earnings in 2011. Table 2. (2012). http://www.bls.gov/cps /cpswom2011.pdf.

[22] U.S. Bureau of Labor Statistics, U.S. Department of Labor. "Median usual weekly earnings of full-time wage and salary workers by occupation and sex, 1983 and 2000 annual averages." *Highlights of women's Earnings in 2000.* 8. (2000). http://bls.gov/cps/cpswom2000.pdf.

[23] U.S. Glass Ceiling Commission. "Glass Ceiling Commission: Good for Business Making Full Use of the Nation's Human Capitol." (March 1995). http://digitalcommons.ilr.cornell.edu /cgi/viewcontent.cgi?article=1118&context=keyworkplace.

[24] Bureau of Labor Statistics, U.S. Department of Labor. "Median usual weekly earnings of full-time wage and salary workers, by detailed occupation and sex, 2011 annual averages." *Highlights of Women's Earnings in 2011.* Table 2. (2012). http://www.bls.gov /cps/cpswom2011.pdf.

[25] This included Members of Congress Florence Price Dwyer, Edith Green, Charles Goodell, Elizabeth Kee, Edna Kelly, Catherine May, Maurine Neuberger, Carlton Sickles, and Leonor K. Sullivan. Also in attendance were Vice President Lyndon B. Johnson, Assistant Labor Secretary and Director of the Women's Bureau Esther Peterson, former Women's Bureau Director Mary Anderson, and leaders from women's organizations and labor unions, including National Federation of Business and Professional Women President Dr. Minnie Miles, National Council of Negro Women President Dr. Dorothy Height, National Council of Jewish Women President Pearl Larner Willen, YWCA Director Ethlyn Christensen, United Auto Workers Women's Director Caroline Davis, AFL-CIO Legislative Director Andrew Biemiller, and General Federation of Women's Clubs Legislative Director Mary M. Chittenden.

[26] Kennedy, John F. "Remarks Upon Signing the Equal Pay Act." *The American Presidency Project.* (1963). http://www.presidency

[27] Bureau of Labor Statistics, U.S. Department of Labor. "Labor Force Participation: 75 Years of Change, 1950-98, and 1998-2025." (1999). http://www.bls.gov/mlr/1999/12/art1full.pdf.

[28] Harrison, Cynthia. "The Equal Pay Act of 1963: Compromise and Victory." *On Account of Sex: The Politics of Women's Issues 1945-1968.* 89-108. (1988).

[29] U.S. Government Printing Office. "American Women: Report of the President's Commission on the Status of Women (1963)."

[30] 110 Cong. Rec. 2577-2584 (1964).

[31] Goodman, B. & Wagner, P.M. "Makers: Women Who Make America." *Public Broadcasting System (PBS).* (2013) http://www.pbs.org/makers/home/.

[32] Goodman, B. & Wagner, P.M. "Makers: Women Who Make America." *Public Broadcasting System (PBS).* (2013) http://www.pbs.org/makers/home/.

[33] Frankel, M. *Tighter Rules on Job Prejudice Against Women Issued by U.S,* N.Y. Times, June 10, 1970.

[34] Herman, A. M., & Castro, I. L. U.S. Department of Labor. "Equal Pay: A Thirty-Five Year Perspective." 51. (1998).

[35] 29 CFR § 541.0.

[36] Equal Employment Opportunity Commission. "Timeline of Important EEOC Events." http://www.eeoc.gov/youth/history

[37] Bureau of Labor Statistics, U.S. Department of Labor. "Labor Force Participation: 75 Years of Change, 1950-98, and 1998-2025." (1999). http://www.bls.gov/mlr/1999/12/art1full.pdf.

[38] Herman, A. M., & Castro, I. L. U.S. Department of Labor. "Equal Pay: A Thirty-Five Year Perspective." Appendix A, Table 1. (1998).

[39] Herman, A. M., & Castro, I. L. U.S. Department of Labor. "Equal Pay: A Thirty-Five Year Perspective." 19. (1998).

[40] Bureau of Labor Statistics, U.S. Department of Labor. "Labor force participation rates by sex, race, and Hispanic or Latino ethnicity, 1972-2009 annual averages." *Labor Force Characteristics by Race and ethnicity, 2009.* (2010). http://www.bls.gov/cps/cpsrace2009.pdf.

[41] B.I.G. Enterprises, Inc. and the Institute for Women's Policy Research. "An analysis of pay disparities between women and men by selected demographic characteristics, 1960 to 2010." *White Paper, Prepared for the U.S. Department of Labor, Women's Bureau.* (2012).

[42] Herman, A. M., & Castro, I. L. U.S. Department of Labor. "Equal Pay: A Thirty-Five Year Perspective." Appendix A, Table 2. (1998).

[43] Herman, A. M., & Castro, I. L. U.S. Department of Labor. "Equal Pay: A Thirty-Five Year Perspective." 19. (1998).

[44] Herman, A. M., & Castro, I. L. U.S. Department of Labor. "Equal Pay: A Thirty-Five Year Perspective." Appendix B, Table 1. (1998).

[45] Herman, A. M., & Castro, I. L. U.S. Department of Labor. "Equal Pay: A Thirty-Five Year Perspective." Appendix A, Table 3. (1998).

[46] U.S. Department of Labor. "Women's History/Our History: The Remarkable Bessie Margolin," *DOL News Brief, March 14, 2013.* http://www.dol.gov/sec/newsletter/2013/20130314.htm; Schultz v. Wheaton Glass Co., 421 F.2d 259 (3d Cir. 1970), cert. denied 398 U.S. 905 (1970).

[47] Corning Glass Works v. Brennan, 417 U.S. 188 (1974).

[48] Herman, A. M., & Castro, I. L. U.S. Department of Labor. "Equal Pay: A Thirty-Five Year Perspective." 52. (1998).

[49] U.S. Census Bureau. "Income, Poverty, and Health Insurance Coverage in the United States: 2011." 48, Table A4. (2012). http://www.census.gov/prod/2012pubs/p60-243.pdf.

[50] County of Washington v. Gunther, 452 U.S. 161 (1981).

[51] National Committee on Pay Equity. "Questions and Answers on Pay Equity." (2013). http://www.payequity.org/info-Q&A.html.

[52] Equal Employment Opportunity Commission. "Policy Guidance on Current Issues of Sexual Harassment." (1990). http://www.eeoc.gov/policy Meritor Savings Bank v. Vinson, 477 U.S. 57 (1986).

[53] U.S. Department of Labor. "The Federal Glass Ceiling Commission, A Solid Investment: Making Full Use of the Nation's Human Capitol." (March 1985). http://www.dol.gov/oasam/programs/history

[54] U.S. Department of Labor. "Wage and Hour Division, The Family and Medical Leave Act Overview." (2013). http://www.dol.gov/whd/fmla/index.htm.

[55] National Center for Education Statistics, U.S. Department of Education. "Degrees Conferred by degree-granting institutions, by level of degree and sex of student: Selected years, 1869-70 through 2019-20." (2010). http://nces.ed.gov/pubs2011/2011015 3b.pdf.

[56] National Center for Education Statistics, U.S. Department of Education. "Degrees Conferred by degree-granting institutions, by level of degree and sex of student: Selected years, 1869-70 through 2019-20." (2010). http://nces.ed.gov/pubs2011/20110153b.pdf.

[57] Bureau of Labor Statistics, U.S. Department of Labor. "Median usual weekly earnings of full-time wage and salary workers 25 years and older, in constant (2011) dollars, by sex and educational attainment, 1979-2011 annual averages." *Highlights of Women's Earnings in 2011.* 67-68. (2012). http://www.bls.gov/cps/cpswom2011.pdf.

[58] Bureau of Labor Statistics, U.S. Department of Labor. "Median usual weekly earnings of full-time wage and salary workers 25 years and older, in constant (2011) dollars, by sex and educational attainment, 1979-2011 annual averages." *Highlights of Women's Earnings in 2011.* 60. (2012). http://www.bls.gov/cps/cpswom2011.pdf.

[59] Bureau of Labor Statistics, U.S. Department of Labor. "Median usual weekly earnings of full-time wage and salary workers 25 years and older, in constant (2011) dollars, by sex and educational attainment, 1979-2011 annual averages." *Highlights of Women's Earnings in 2011.* 67. (2012). http://www.bls.gov/cps/cpswom2011.pdf.

[60] Bureau of Labor Statistics, U.S. Department of Labor. "Civilian labor force participation rates by age, sex, race, and ethnicity, 1990, 2000, 2010, and projected 2020." (2012). http://www.bls.gov/emp/eptable303.htm.

[61] U.S. Census Bureau. "Employment status of women by marital status and presence and age of children: 1970 to 2009." (2012). http://www.census.gov/compendia/statab/2012/tables/12s0599.pdf.

[62] U.S. Census Bureau. "Employment status of women by marital status and presence and age of children: 1970 to 2009." (2012). http://www.census.gov/compendia/statab/2012/tables/12s0599.pdf.

[63] U.S. Census Bureau. "Civilian labor force- percent distribution by sex and age: 1980 to 2010." (2012). http://www.census.gov/compendia/statab/2012/tables/12s0592.pdf.

[64] Bureau of Labor Statistics, U.S. Department of Labor. "Contribution of wives' earnings to family income, 1970- 2010." *Women in the Labor Force: A Databook.* 81. (2013). http://www.bls.gov/cps/wlf-databook-2012.pdf.

[65] Bureau of Labor Statistics, U.S. Department of Labor. "Wives who earn more than their husbands, 1987-2010." *Women in the Labor Force: A Databook.* 82. (2013). http://www.bls.gov/cps/wlf-databook-2012.pdf.

[66] U.S. Census Bureau. "Full-time, year-round workers by median earnings and sex: 1960 to 2011." *Historical Income Tables.* (2011) http://www.census.gov/hhes/www/income

[67] U.S. Census Bureau. "Money income in the United States: 1996." (1997). https://www.census.gov/prod/3/97pubs/P60-197.PDF.

[68] U.S. Census Bureau. "Women's Earnings as a Percentage of Men's Earnings by Race and Hispanic Origin." *Historical Income Tables, Table P-40.* (2011). http://www.census.gov/hhes/www/income

[69] U.S. Census Bureau. "Income, Poverty, and Health Insurance Coverage in the United States: 2011." 48, Table A4. (2012). http://www.census.gov/prod/2012pubs/p60-243.pdf.

[70] Council of Economic Advisors, The White House. "Explaining Trends in the Gender Wage Gap." (1998). http://clinton4.nara.gov/WH/EOP/CEA/html/gendergap.html.

[71] U.S. Equal Employment Opportunity Commission. EEOC Notice No. 915.002. (October 29, 2007). http://www.eeoc.gov/policy

[72] Advisory Group of Women of Silicon Valley. "Unfinished Business: The Women in Silicon Valley Economy." *Collaborative Economics.* (April 2011). http://www.coecon.com/Reports/Archives/UnfinishedBusiness.pdf.

[73] National Center for Veterans Analysis and Statistics, U.S. Department of Veterans Affairs. *America's Women Veterans, Military Service History and VA Benefit Utilization Statistics.* (November 23, 2011). http://www.va.gov/VETDATA/docs/SpecialReports/Final Womens Report 3 2 12 v 7.pdf.

[74] National Center for Education Statistics, U.S. Department of Education. "Degrees Conferred by degree-granting institutions, by level of degree and sex of student: Selected years, 1869-70 through 2019-20." (2010). http://nces.ed.gov/pubs2011/20110153b.pdf.

[75] Bureau of Labor Statistics, U.S. Department of Labor. "Median usual weekly earnings of full-time wage and salary workers 25 years and over by sex, race, Hispanic or Latino ethnicity, and educational attainment, annual averages 1979-2011." (unpublished table).

[76] U.S. Census Bureau. "Income, poverty, and health insurance coverage in the United States: 2011." 48, Table A-4. (2012). http://www.census.gov/prod/2012pubs/p60-243.pdf.

[77] U.S. Census Bureau. "Educational Attainment--Full-Time, Year-Round Workers 25 Years Old and Over by Median Earnings and Sex: 1991 to 2011." *Historical Income Tables.* (2011). http://www.census.gov/hhes/www/income

[78] U.S. Census Bureau. "Income, poverty, and health insurance coverage in the United states: 2011." 48, TABLE A4. (2012). http://www.census.gov/prod/2012pubs/p60-243.pdf.

[79] Bureau of Labor Statistics, U.S. Department of Labor. "Civilian labor force participation rates by age, sex, race, and ethnicity, 1990, 2000, 2010, and projected 2020." (2012). http://www.bls.gov/emp/ep table 303.htm.

[80] Bureau of Labor Statistics, U.S. Department of Labor. "Unpublished marital and family tables." *Current Population Survey.* 49, Table 3.

[81] Bureau of Labor Statistics, U.S. Department of Labor. "Employment status of the civilian noninstitutional population by sex, age, presence and age of youngest child, marital status, race, and Hispanic origin, March 2010." *Current Population Survey.* 25, Table 3. (2010).

[82] Bureau of Labor Statistics, U.S. Department of Labor. "Employment status of women by presence and age of youngest child, marital status, race, and Hispanic or Latino ethnicity, March 2010." *Women In the Labor Force: A Databook.* 15, Table 6. (2011). http://bls.gov/cps/wlf-databook-2011.pdf.

[83] U.S. Census Bureau. "Civilian Labor Force- Percent Distribution by sex and age: 1980 to 2010." (2012). http://www.census.gov/compendia/statab/2012/tables/12s0592.pdf.

[84] Bureau of Labor Statistics, U.S. Department of Labor. "Contribution of wives' earnings to family income, 1970- 2010." *Women in the Labor Force: A Databook.* 81. (2013). http://www.bls.gov/cps/wlf-databook-2012.pdf.

[85] Bureau of Labor Statistics, U.S. Department of Labor. "Wives who earn more than their husbands." *Women in the Labor Force: A Databook.* 82. (2013). http://www.bls.gov /cps/wlf-databook-2012.pdf.

[86] Equal Employment Opportunity Commission. "Equal Pay Act Charges (includes concurrent charges with Title VII, ADEA and ADA) FY 1997- FY 2012." (2013). http://www.eeoc.gov/eeoc/statistics

[87] Bureau of Labor Statistics, U.S. Department of Labor. "More Couples are Working Longer," *Working in the 21st Century: Chartbook.* (2013). http://www.bls.gov/opub /working/page17b.htm.

[88] Equal Employment Opportunity Commission. "Employer Best Practices for Workers With Caregiving Responsibilities." (2007). http://www.eeoc.gov/policy

[89] Ledbetter v. Goodyear Tire & Rubber Co., 550 U.S. 618 (2007).

[90] *TAP Talks with Lilly Ledbetter.* The American Prospect, April 23, 2008. http://www.prospect.org/cs/articles?article=tap_talks_with_lilly_ledbetter.

[91] National Equal Pay Enforcement Task Force. "National Equal Pay Enforcement Task Force." *The White House.* . (2010). http://www.whitehouse.gov/sites/default/files/rssviewe r/equalpaytaskforce.pdf.

[92] In 2010, women on average earned 81 cents for every dollar earned by a man. Bureau of Labor Statistics, U.S. Department of Labor. *Women at Work.* (2011). In 2011 and 2012, that figure fluctuated between 80 and 82 cents. Bureau of Labor Statistics, U.S. Department of Labor. "Labor Force Statistics from Current Population Survey." *Current Population Survey.*

http://www.bls.gov/cps/earnings Updated quarterly CPS earnings figures by demographics by quarter through the end of 2012 *available at* http://www.bls.gov/news.release /wkyeng.t01.htm.

[93] U.S. Census Bureau. "Income, Poverty and Health Insurance Coverage in the United States." *Current Population Reports 2011.* (Sept. 2012). http://www.census.gov/prod/2012pubs /p60-243.pdf.

[94] Calculated from Bureau of Labor Statistics CPS data, *available at* http://www.bls.gov/cps /cpsrace2011.pdf.

[95] A March 2011 White House report entitled "Women in America: Indicators of Social and Economic Well-Being," found that while earnings for women and men typically increase with higher levels of education, male-female pay gap persists at all levels of education for full-time workers (35 or more hours per week), according to 2009 Bureau of Labor Statistics wage data. Potentially non-discriminatory factors can explain some of the gender wage differences. Even so, after controlling for differences in skills and job characteristics, women still earn less than men. Council of Economic Advisors. "Explaining Trends in the Gender Wage Gap." (June 1998); *see also,* Hegewisch, A., Williams, C., Harbin, V. *The Gender Wage Gap by Occupation.* (2012). (women's median earnings less than men in virtually all occupations); LoSasso, A. T., et al. "The $16,819 Pay Gap For Newly Trained Physicians: The Unexplained Trend Of Men Earning More Than Women." *30 Health Affairs 193.* (2011). Ultimately, the research literature still finds an unexplained gap exists even after accounting for potential explanations, and finds that the narrowing of the pay gap for women has slowed since the 1980s. Jacobsen, J.P. *The Economics of Gender.* 44. (2007); Blau, F.D. & Kahn, L.M. "The U.S. gender pay gap in the 1990s: slowing convergence." *60 Industrial and Labor Relations Review 45.* (2006). In addition to the gender pay gap, scholars have found race and ethnicity-based pay gaps that put workers of color at a disadvantage. Altonji, J.G. and Blank, R. M. "Race and Gender in the Labor Market," in *Handbook of Labor Economics* (Ashenfelter, O. and Card, D., eds.). 3143. (1999).

[96] Bureau of Labor Statistics, U.S. Department of Labor. "Women in the Labor Force: A Databook" *BLS Reports.* 12- 13, Table 3. (2013). http://www.bls.gov/cps/wlf-databook-2012.pdf.

[97] Bureau of Labor Statistics, U.S. Department of Labor. "Women in the Labor Force: A Databook" *BLS Reports.* 1; 13-15, Table 4. (2013). http://www.bls.gov/cps/wlf-databook-2012.pdf.

[98] National Center for Education Statistics, U.S. Department of Education. "Bachelor's, master's, and doctor's degrees conferred by degree-granting institutions, by sex of student and discipline division: 2009-10." U.S. *Digest of Education Statistics.* Table 290. (2011). http://nces.ed.gov/programs/digest/d11/tables/dt11290.asp.

[99] Bureau of Labor Statistics, U.S. Department of Labor. "Women in the Labor Force: A Databook, 2012." *BLS Reports.* (2013). http://www.bls.gov/cps/wlf-databook-2012.pdf.

[100] Goldin, C. *Understanding the Gender Gap: An Economic History of American Women* (1990).

[101] CEA calculations based on Current Population Survey.

[102] Women's Bureau, U.S. Department of Labor. "20 Leading Occupations of Employed Women, 2010." (2010). http://www.dol.gov/wb/factsheets/20lead2010.htm.

[103] Women's Bureau, U.S. Department of Labor. "Nontraditional Occupations of Employed Women in 2010." (2010). http://www.dol.gov/wb/stats/NontraJobs 2010.htm.

[104] Herman, A. M., & Castro, I. L. U.S. Department of Labor. "Equal Pay: A Thirty-Five Year Perspective." 18. (1998).

[105] Blau, F.D., Brummund, P. and Yung-Hsu Liu, A. "Trends in Occupational Segregation by Gender 1970-2009: Adjusting for the Impact of Changes in the Occupational Coding System." *NBER Working Paper*. (2012).

[106] U.S. Department of Commerce, Economics and Statistics Administration. "Women in STEM: A Gender Gap to Innovation." (August 2011).

[107] U.S. Department of Veterans Affairs. "America's Women: Past, Present and Future, (2007)." http://www.va.gov/VETDATA/docs/SpecialReports/Womenveterans Past Present Future 9-30-07a.pdf.

[108] U.S. Census Bureau. "Facts for Features: Women's History Month." *Newsroom*. (2013). *http://www.census.gov/newsroom/releases/archives/factsforfeaturesspecialeditions/cb13-ff04.html*.

[109] Alliance for National Defense. "Women in Combat." *Issue Paper*. http://www.4military women.org/WomeninCombat.htm.

[110] Becker, G. *The Economics of Discrimination*. (1957); Goldin, C. "A Pollution Theory of Discrimination: Male and Female Differences in Occupations and Earnings." *NBER Working Paper*. (2002).

[111] Mincer, J. and Polachek, S. "Family Investments in Human Capital: Earnings of Women." *Journal of Political Economy* 82:2. (1974).

[112] Blau, F.D., Ferber, M.A., Winkler, A.E. *The Economics of Women, Men, and Work (6th Edition)*. (2010).

[113] Weinberger, Catherine J. "An Economist's Perspective on Women in the IT Workforce." *Encyclopedia of Gender and Information Technology, Information Science Publishing (Idea Group)*. (2006).

[114] Hunt, J. "Why do Women Leave Science and Engineering?" *NBER Working Paper*. (2010).

[115] U.S. Bureau of Labor Statistics, U.S. Department of Labor. "Employed persons by occupation, sex and age." *Current Population Survey*. (2013). http://www.bls.gov /cps/cpsaat09.htm.

[116] Institute for Women's Policy Research. "New Study: Men Earn More Than Women Within Nearly All the Most Common Occupations." (2012). http://www.iwpr.org/press-room/press-releases/new-study-men-earn-morethan-women-within-nearly-all-the-most-common-occupations. In a recent review of 2010 Census data, Bloomberg found only one of 285 major occupations where women's median pay was higher than that of men – personal care and service workers. Bass, F. Shining Shoes Best Way Wall Street Women Outearn Men, Bloomberg. (Mar. 16, 2012). *Available at* http://www.bloomberg.com/news /2012-03-16/shining-shoes-best-way-wall-street-womenoutearn-men.html

[117] LoSasso, A. T., et al. "The $16,819 Pay Gap For Newly Trained Physicians: The Unexplained Trend Of Men Earning More Than Women." *30 Health Affairs 193*. (2011). *Available at* http://content.healthaffairs.org/content/30/2/193.abstract. Catalyst also reviewed 2011 government data showing a gender pay gap for women lawyers, and that data confirms that the gap exists for a range of professional and technical occupations. Bureau of Labor Statistics, U.S. Department of Labor. "Median weekly earnings of full-time wage and salary workers by detailed occupation and sex." (2012). http://www.bls.gov/cps/cpsaat39.pdf.

[118] Bureau of Labor Statistics, U.S. Department of Labor. "Median weekly earnings of full-time wage and salary workers by detailed occupation and sex." (2012). http://www.bls.gov/cps/cpsaat39.pdf; LoSasso, A. T., et al. "The $16,819 Pay Gap For Newly Trained Physicians: The Unexplained Trend Of Men Earning More Than Women."

30 Health Affairs 193. (2011). *Available at* http://content.healthaffairs.org /content/30/2/193.abstract.

[119] Benard, S., Paik, I., and Correll, S. J. "Cognitive Bias and the Motherhood Penalty." *59 Hastings L.J. 1359.* (2007 2008); Benard, S., Paik, I., and Correll, S. J. "Getting a Job: Is There a Motherhood Penalty?" 112 *Am. J. of Sociology 5.* (March 2007). http:/gender.stanford.edu/sites/default/files/motherhoodpenalty.pdf.

[120] Office of the Press Secretary. "Remarks by the President in the State of the Union Address." *The White House.* (2010). http://www.whitehouse.gov/the-press-office/remarks-president

[121] These include Title VII of the Civil Rights Act of 1964 (enforced by the EEOC, DOJ and OPM), the Equal Pay Act (enforced by EEOC and OPM), and Executive Order 11246 (enforced by DOL).

[122] Sutphen, M. "Putting Washington at the Service of the Middle Class." *The White House Rural Council.* (2010). http://www.whitehouse.gov/blog/2010/01/27/putting-washington-service-middle-class.

[123] National Equal Pay Enforcement Task Force. "National Equal Pay Enforcement Task Force." *The White House.* (2010). http://www.whitehouse.gov/sites/default/files/rss viewer/equal pay task force.pdf.

[124] Office of the Vice President. "Vice President Biden Holds Middle Class Task Force Event on Work and Family." *The White House.* (2010). http://www.whitehouse.gov/the-press-office/vice-president-task-force-event-work-and-family.

[125] Both the Notice of Rescission and the new guidance information can be found at http:www.dol.gov/ofccp/compguidance.

[126] Division of Behavioral and Social Sciences and Education. "Measuring and Collecting Pay Information from U.S. Employers by Gender, Race, and National Origin" *The National Academies.* (2010). http://www8.nationalacademies.org/cp/projectview.aspx?key=49344.

[127] The National Acadamies Press. "Collecting Compensation Data from Employers." *National Acadamies of Sciences.* (2012). http://www.nap.edu/catalog.php?recordid=13496.

[128] 76 Fed. Reg. 49398 (Aug. 10, 2011).

[129] U.S. Department of Labor. "Equal Pay." (2012). http://www.dol.gov/equalpay/

[130] The Women's Bureau, U.S. Department of Labor. "Equal Pay App Challenge: Final Results and Prize Winners." (2012). http://www.dol.gov/equalpay/apps-winners.htm.

[131] The White House. "Accomplishments of the Equal Pay Task Force: Fighting for Fair Pay in the Workplace." (April 2012). www.whitehouse.gov/...equalpaytaskforce.pdf.

[132] White House Council on Women and Girls,."The Key to an Economy Built to Last." (April 2012). http://www.whitehouse.gov/sites/default/files/email-files/womens_report_final_for_ print.pdf.

[133] See Appendix for methods used to calculate new poverty figures.

[134] Hsieh, C., Hurst, E. Jones, C. I., Klenow, P. J. "The Allocation of Talent and U.S. Economic Growth." *NBER Working Paper.* (2013).

APPENDIX: METHODS USED TO COMPUTE NEW POVERTY RATES

To simulate what would happen if we increased female earnings, we used data from the2012 March Annual Social and Economic Supplement to the Current Population Survey (CPS). Using the same poverty universe incorporated by the Census Bureau (http://www.census.gov/prod /2012pubs/p60- 243.pdf), we increased the annual earnings of working women age 18 and over by 10 percent. Doing so would lift nearly 1.3 million individuals out of poverty (Table A1, column 5). It would also lift more than 700,000 people out of poverty who live in single female-headed families with children. About 550,000 children would be brought out of poverty under such an exercise, with over 400,000 children coming from families with single mothers.

Table A1. Individuals and Children in Poverty Before and After Increasing Female Earnings 10% (Number in Thousands)

	Original		New		Difference	
	Number in Poverty	Percent	Number in Poverty	Percent	Number	Percent
		Individuals				
Total Individuals	46,247	15.0	44,952	14.6	1,295	0.4
Individuals in Families with Children						
Under 18	27,505	18.5	26,535	17.8	969	0.7
Female Reference Person Family	15,193	42.7	14,460	40.7	733	2.1
Husband-Wife Family	10,434	9.9	10,203	9.7	231	0.2
Individuals in Families with No						
Children Under 18	18,742	11.8	18,417	11.6	325,735	0.2
		Children				
Children in Families with Children						
Under 18	15,963	21.7	15,416	21.0	547	0.7
Female Reference Person Family	9,525	46.2	9,086	44.1	440	2.1
Husband-Wife Family	5,320	11.0	5,214	10.8	106	0.2

Note: Families include related and unrelated subfamilies Source: Current Population Survey, March 2012

In: The Equal Pay Act, Fifty Years on   ISBN: 978-1-63463-730-5
Editor: Suzanna Cross   © 2015 Nova Science Publishers, Inc.

Chapter 2

GOVERNMENTWIDE STRATEGY ON ADVANCING PAY EQUALITY IN THE FEDERAL GOVERNMENT*

U.S. Office of Personnel Management

EXECUTIVE SUMMARY

President's Memorandum. On May 10, 2013, President Obama signed a memorandum to the heads of executive departments and agencies (agencies) on Advancing Pay Equality in the Federal Government and Learning from Successful Practices. This memorandum directed the Director of the U.S. Office of Personnel Management (OPM) to submit to the President a Governmentwide strategy to address any gender pay gap in the Federal workforce. This strategy must include—

- An analysis of whether changes to the General Schedule (GS) classification system would assist in addressing any gender pay gap;
- Proposed guidance to agencies to promote greater transparency regarding starting salaries; and
- Recommendations for additional administrative or legislative actions or studies.

---

* This is an edited, reformatted and augmented version of report number ES/PL/PA-2014-05, issued April 2014.

OPM Collection of Information from Agencies. To facilitate the development of a Governmentwide strategy, the President's memorandum required each agency to provide OPM information on and an analysis of specific matters related to starting salaries, promotions, and agency-specific policies and best practices. On May 10, 2013, OPM issued a memorandum to agencies providing guidance on reviewing their pay and promotion policies and practices in accordance with the President's memorandum. Our guidance explained that the focus of the review was on policies and practices on starting salaries and promotions for GS employees and equivalent-level white-collar employees in other pay systems. This policy review covered approximately 1.7 million employees (including 1.3 million GS employees) of the approximately 2.1 million Federal employees. We received responses from 51 agencies, including all cabinet-level departments.

OPM Data Analysis. To assist in developing a Governmentwide strategy to address any gender pay issues, we analyzed workforce data reported by agencies to OPM central data systems in each of 3 years—1992, 2002, and 2012. We primarily focused our data analysis efforts on white-collar employees. We produced three overall types of statistical reports: workforce snapshot data, regression-decomposition data analysis, and dynamic data on certain personnel actions such as use of pay-setting flexibilities for new hires and promotion and quality step increase actions. We also collected data on various factors, such as occupation, age, agency, education level, length of service, and supervisory status. With respect to occupation, 37 occupational groups were used in most analyses.

Workforce Changes. We found that during the 20-year period from 1992 to 2012, the Federal Government workforce has undergone dramatic demographic changes. For example, there have been large shifts in the distribution of employees by occupational category and education level. Simultaneously, there have been significant shifts in the male-female distribution across occupations and education levels. In terms of general occupational category (Professional-Administrative-Technical-Clerical-Other or "PATCO"), there has been a large reduction in Clerical employees and a large increase in Administrative employees. The percentage of females in Professional jobs increased significantly. In terms of education level, the percentage of employees and the percentage of females with a Bachelor Degree or higher increased significantly.

OPM Data Findings. Some additional key data findings from OPM's analysis are highlighted below:

- Over the study years (1992-2002-2012), the gender pay gap has dramatically shrunk from about 30 percent to 13 percent (for All White Collar) and to 11 percent (for GS only).
- The differences in the distribution of males and females across occupational categories appear to explain much of the pay gap. This finding was reinforced by multivariate regression and decomposition analysis, which showed that 70 percent of the White Collar pay gap was explained by the factors used in our analysis and that the occupational factor accounted for 76 percent of the explained portion of the gap in 2012. A separate analysis of the GS population produced similar results—67 percent of the gap was explained in 2012, with 93 percent of that explained portion attributable to the occupational factor. While occupational distribution explains much of the pay gap, we are not ruling out the possibility that discriminatory influences played a role in occupational distribution.
- The regression and decomposition analysis shows that the unexplained portion of the pay gap in 2012 was 30 percent of the total pay gap for All White Collar and 33 percent of the total pay gap for the GS (less than 4 percentage points). (This unexplained portion could be attributable to factors that may or may not be discriminatory that were not accounted for in our analysis (e.g., non-Federal work experience, personal obligations).)
- The pay gap was smaller in younger age groups. Pay gaps at different ages may reflect the differences in occupational distribution at those ages.
- In 2012, pay gaps were found at all education levels, almost all in the 8-10 percent range.
- In 2012, for supervisors and managers, the average female salary was 95.6 percent of the average male salary; however, females made up only 36 percent of supervisors and managers. Among members of the Senior Executive Service (SES), the female salary percentage was 99.2 percent; however, females made up only 33 percent of SES members.
- When we examined pay gaps by grade level for the GS population, we found that there was no significant gap between female and male salaries. However, more females were found in lower grades, which may be a reflection of differences in occupational distribution.

- For GS employees, a discretionary authority to set pay for new hires above the step 1 minimum rate was used more frequently (on a percentage basis) for males than females in all 3 study years. Closer analysis revealed that these actions are most heavily used in three occupational categories that are male-dominated, which affected the overall usage rates.
- For GS employees, females received out-of-cycle "quality" step increases for outstanding performance more frequently (on a percentage basis) than males in all 3 study years.
- Starting salaries were lower for females than males, on average, in all 3 years—roughly 10 percent lower in 2012. When we analyzed White Collar starting salaries for the 37 more-specific occupational categories in 2012, we found that female starting salaries exceeded male starting salaries for 14 categories and were within 5 percent of male starting salaries for another 12 categories. Only 4 categories had pay gaps of more than 10 percent (no more than 12 percent). Differences in occupational distribution between males and females appear to explain much of the overall starting salary pay gap. When we examined GS starting salaries by GS grade level, we found that male and female average starting salaries were quite close in all three years.
- Promotions were received more frequently (on a percentage basis) by females than males in all 3 study years. When we examined White Collar promotion rates for the 37 more-specific occupational categories in 2012, we found that the female promotion rate exceeded the male rate for 27 of 37 categories.

Governmentwide Strategy. The President's memorandum requires OPM to develop a Governmentwide strategy to address any gender pay gap in the Federal Government to include an analysis of the GS classification system, proposed guidance to promote greater starting salary transparency, and recommendations for additional administrative or legislative actions or studies. The following summarizes OPM's recommended strategies.

Analysis of GS Classification System. After a comprehensive review of agency reports, there were no indicators that changes to the GS classification system would assist in addressing any gender pay gap. There was no evidence provided by agencies that the law (i.e., 5 U.S.C. chapter 51), regulations (i.e., 5 CFR part 511), and OPM's policies and standards on GS classification may be affecting gender pay equality. In fact, adherence to the principle of equal pay for equal work is evident based on the agency data collected and reviewed for this study. OPM will work with agencies to review their internal classification policies and application of the GS classification system in compliance with the principle of equal pay for substantially equal work. Additionally, OPM will assist agencies, in exercising their delegated classification authority, in collecting metrics and other relevant agency data to examine classification practices based on a variety of factors, including gender analysis by occupation. In support, OPM will work with agencies to review their application of classification policies and identify their need for guidance and/or training to support human resources (HR) professionals in the application of the GS classification system, and provide tools and guidance on key classification policy issues. OPM currently hosts a quarterly Classification Policy Forum with agency classification leads. We will use this forum to discuss and identify possible gender pay gap issues as they pertain to classification practices. We will also use the forum to champion agency best practices regarding gender pay equality, and to provide support to agencies to promote internal agency partnerships that include their HR, Equal Employment Opportunity and Diversity and Inclusion Offices with the common goal of gender pay equality.

Proposed Guidance to Promote Greater Starting Salary Transparency. OPM will work with agencies to ensure GS equivalent-level salary tables or rate ranges are made available to job candidates to promote greater transparency regarding starting salaries. OPM posts GS and other Governmentwide pay tables that OPM administers on its public website. Agencies are required by law and regulation to post starting pay on competitive job announcements. However, not all agencies make all of their pay tables or rate ranges for their GS equivalent-level employees available to the public. Ensuring agencies post such information on their websites would provide transparency regarding non-GS pay rates for all job candidates.

OPM will also explore ways to ensure pay-setting options and other salary information is made readily available to job candidates as another way to promote greater transparency regarding starting salaries. OPM has fact sheets on pay-setting options for GS employees on its website. We will explore whether to provide links to these fact sheets and other information on starting salaries for GS positions on USAJOBS or on OPM's public website. OPM will work with agencies to ensure that other salary information is also made available to all job candidates for GS and non-GS pay systems.

Additional Administrative or Legislative Actions or Studies. OPM developed five recommendations for additional administrative actions or studies that should be undertaken to address the gender pay gap. First, we will work with agencies to clarify the range of GS pay-setting flexibility and share best practices on setting starting salaries in gender-neutral ways. Some of the best practices agencies shared with OPM are setting pay based on specific criteria for certain occupations and using compensation panels that do not include hiring managers to recommend the use of pay flexibilities.

Second, we will develop guidance for agencies to conduct their own gender data analyses, review their starting salary trends and use of pay-setting flexibilities, and review their promotion data to determine if gender equity issues are apparent so that they can develop approaches to address any issues. Most agencies reported that they do not review their use of pay-setting flexibilities on a periodic basis to examine the gender distribution of employees for which the authorities are used. Most reports also did not indicate that agencies perform other types of pay or promotion data analyses by gender on a routine basis.

Third, we will explore the need to conduct additional Governmentwide statistical analyses to obtain a better understanding of gender pay trends for specific categories of employees not covered by OPM's initial data review.

Fourth, we will work with agencies to share best practices and develop recruitment and outreach strategies for growing female populations in occupations where they are underrepresented—e.g., science, technology, engineering, and mathematics (STEM) and other nontraditional jobs; and supervisory and managerial jobs, as part of an overall recruitment plan. OPM will continue to work with partners from the private and public sector to increase awareness of Federal STEM occupations, promote Federal careers, education, and training opportunities to women and minorities. OPM will continue to provide training for agency HR professionals, agency hiring managers, and Special Programs Coordinators on how to conduct strategic recruitment for mission-critical occupations and hard-to-find skills, including STEM. OPM plans to promote agency "best practices" on attracting and recruiting a diverse workforce in our newly created Recruiting Policy suite on HR University (*hru.gov/recruiting/resources.aspx*). OPM is creating video tutorials for job seekers available on USAJOBS' YouTube to educate them on the Federal hiring process and hiring programs such as the Pathways Programs for students and recent graduates. OPM will expand social media outreach to include groups and resources directed to women to reach broader, targeted audiences and to raise awareness of agencies' mission and career opportunities. OPM will seek out collaborative recruiting relationships with colleges and universities, technical and trade schools, professional associations, and student organizations to improve outreach effectiveness and to broaden access to employment opportunities for women, as part of an overall outreach strategy.

Fifth, we will work with agencies to share best practices and develop guidance for when to consider work schedule changes to part-time. This may include exploring with agencies the feasibility of establishing more positions as part-time job sharing positions—, i.e., two or more part-time employees performing the work of one full-time position, to increase the number of promotional opportunities for part-time employees. Positions established as part-time are a very small percentage of Federal positions due to agency workloads and organizational needs. Every reporting agency also considers these factors when deciding employee requests for part-time work schedules. Although agencies reported that part-time employees are considered for promotions on the same basis as full-time employees, additional study is needed to determine the percentage of those employees who must change to a full-time schedule if selected. Depending on the basis for the part-time schedule, part-time employees may be reluctant to accept the higher graded position if doing so would require changing to a full-time schedule. Increasing the number of job-sharing opportunities at various grade levels may provide additional promotion opportunities for females since they work a higher percentage of part-time schedules than males.

DETAILED REPORT

I. President's Memorandum

On May 10, 2013, President Obama signed a memorandum to the heads of executive departments and agencies (agencies) on Advancing Pay Equality in the Federal Government and Learning from Successful Practices.[1] This memorandum directed the Director of OPM to submit to the President a Governmentwide strategy to address any gender pay gap in the Federal workforce. This strategy must include—

- An analysis of whether changes to the General Schedule (GS) classification system would assist in addressing any gender pay gap;
- Proposed guidance to agencies to promote greater transparency regarding starting salaries; and

- Recommendations for additional administrative or legislative actions or studies.

To facilitate the development of a Governmentwide strategy, the President's memorandum required each agency to provide OPM information on and an analysis of the following matters:

- All agency-specific policies and practices for setting starting salaries for new employees;
- All agency-specific policies and practices that may affect the salaries of individuals who are returning to the workplace after having taken extended time off from their careers (for example, those who served as full-time caregivers to children or other family members);
- All agency-specific policies and practices for evaluating individuals regarding promotions, particularly individuals who work part-time schedules (for example, those who serve as caregivers to children or other family members);
- Any additional agency-specific policies or practices that may be affecting gender pay equality; and
- Any best practices the agency has employed to improve gender pay equality.

The President's memorandum also directed OPM to provide guidance to agencies on reviewing their pay and promotion policies and practices and on the scope of their review.

II. OPM's Request for Information

A. OPM's Guidance Memorandum

On May 10, 2013, OPM issued a memorandum to heads of executive departments and agencies providing guidance on reviewing their pay and promotion policies and practices in accordance with the President's memorandum.[2] OPM's guidance explained that the focus of the review was on agency policies and practices on starting salaries and promotions for GS employees and equivalent-level employees in other pay systems.[3] This policy review covered approximately 1.7 million of the approximately 2.1 million

Federal employees (or about 81 percent of the workforce). Approximately 1.3 million of the 1.7 million Federal employees are under the GS system (or about 62 percent of the workforce). We also limited the reviews to pay systems that cover more than 100 employees in a given agency, though we encouraged agencies not meeting this threshold to identify any policies or practices that may contribute to gender pay inequality and to share their findings and views with OPM. We did not ask agencies to conduct a data analysis, but we did ask for information (e.g., legal authority, number of employees, etc.) for any "equivalent-level" pay systems covered by an agency's review.

The OPM memorandum provided a list of questions that directly related to the requirements in the President's memorandum to help guide agencies in reviewing their pay and promotion policies and practices and reporting to OPM. The memorandum asked questions regarding—

- Information agencies provide to job applicants or candidates on pay-setting flexibilities and typical starting salaries, whether agencies periodically review their use of pay flexibilities by gender, and, for GS equivalent-level systems, whether salary ranges and tables are available to the general public. These questions were designed to help identify any guidance that may be needed to promote greater transparency regarding starting salaries.
- Use of pay flexibilities (such as the GS superior qualifications and special needs pay-setting authority, GS maximum payable rate rule, and similar flexibilities in equivalent-level systems). These questions were designed to elicit information on agency policies and practices for setting starting salaries for new employees and salaries for individuals who are returning to the workplace after having taken extended time off from their careers.
- Promotion policies and practices. These questions were designed to help gain an understanding for how agencies evaluate individuals for promotions, particularly individuals who work part-time schedules.
- Information on any additional policies or practices in the agency or Governmentwide, including relevant recruitment-related policies and practices and any comments on whether the law, regulations, or policies and standards on GS classification or GS pay setting may be affecting gender pay equality.

- Best practices the agency has employed to improve gender pay equality. Best practices may point to solutions that could be implemented Governmentwide to improve gender pay equality.

B. Agency Reports

OPM received responses from 51 agencies to its May 10, 2013, request for information on pay and promotion policies relating to gender pay equality. This included reports from all cabinet-level and most independent agencies covered by the reporting requirement. See section V. "Governmentwide Strategy" for additional information on the major findings in agency reports that are guiding this strategy.

III. OPM's Data Analysis Process

To assist in developing and supporting a Governmentwide strategy to address any gender pay issues, we extracted and analyzed workforce data reported by agencies to OPM central data systems. We used data reported to OPM's Enterprise Human Resources Integration—Statistical Data Mart (EHRI-SDM) [4] (and its predecessor the Central Personnel Data File (CPDF)) in each of three years—1992, 2002, and 2012—to analyze trends over the last 20 years. Our study population was limited to nonseasonal, full-time, permanent Executive branch employees in a pay status. We primarily focused our data analysis efforts on white-collar employees, consistent with the agency policy review. We also conducted separate analyses of the white-collar General Schedule workforce.[5]

We produced three overall types of statistical reports—

1. Workforce snapshot data. We extracted and analyzed data by gender to obtain a picture of specific workforce characteristics (or a snapshot) in each December of 1992, 2002, and 2012, such as occupation and grade distribution.
2. Multivariate regression and decomposition data analysis. We used a multivariate regression and decomposition statistical analysis method to account for pay differences by gender that may be due to objective factors or characteristics such as occupation, age, or educational background. This method can be used to isolate the portion of any pay

gap that cannot be attributed to identifiable factors or characteristics. We performed this analysis using data for December 1992, December 2002, and December 2012.[6]

3. Workforce dynamic data. We extracted and analyzed data to gain an understanding of any gender differences in certain personnel actions such as use of the superior qualifications and special needs pay setting authority and promotion and quality step increase actions. We examined data for calendar years 1992, 2002, and 2012.

For purposes of conducting data analysis, we relied on factors in the database that describe employee characteristics. The factors included are listed below, along with the number of subpopulations established for each factor:

- Age (6 age ranges)
- Agency (8 groupings plus other)
- Bargaining unit status (3)
- Disability status (4)
- Duty station (50 states, DC, plus other)
- Education level (10)[7]
- Grade level (for GS employees) (15 grades)
- Law enforcement officer status (2)
- Length of service (8 ranges)
- Occupational category #1 (PATCO code) (5)
- Occupational category #2 (37)
- Pay plan (4)
- Race/ethnicity (6)
- Supervisory status (2)
- Veterans status (3)

The 37 occupational groups under Occupational Category #2 are based on combinations of employees' PATCO code[8] and occupational family[9] or series—e.g., 08xx-P for Professional employees in the Engineering and Architecture Job Family. Based on our analysis, we determined that use of the five very broad PATCO categories would prevent us from fully identifying the factors behind gender pay disparities. Inclusion of a more precise measure of occupation does not mean that we are taking a position as to whether or not discrimination is influencing (1) the distribution of males and females across occupational groups or (2) relative grade/pay levels for different occupational groups. Rather we are simply trying to establish what factors most contribute to the gender pay gap. Those factors that have the greatest contributing effect may warrant additional analysis and perhaps corrective measures—to the extent those factors are controllable by the employee or the employer.

IV. DATA ANALYSIS FINDINGS

A. Workforce Changes

During the 20-year period from 1992 to 2012, the Federal Government workforce has undergone dramatic demographic changes. For example, there have been large shifts in the distribution of employees across occupational categories and education levels. Simultaneously, there have been significant shifts in the male-female distribution across occupations and education levels. These shifts are captured by Tables 1 and 2 below. Appendix 1 provides additional data on changes in the composition of the white-collar workforce.

Table 1. Changing Distribution of PATCO Populations and Males/Females within Those Populations - 1992 to 2012 – White Collar (All Pay Plans)

	1992				2012			
PATCO Occup. Category	% of Total	M:F Split	Male % Distrib.	Female % Distrib.	% of Total	M:F Split	Male % Distrib.	Female % Distrib.
Professional	26.5	67:33	34.4	18.2	28.0	55:45	28.6	27.2
Administrative	32.7	60:40	38.1	26.9	43.6	57:43	46.4	40.4
Technical	22.3	43:57	18.7	26.2	18.7	42:58	14.8	23.3
Clerical	15.8	14:86	4.2	28.1	5.3	31:69	3.1	7.9
Other	2.7	90:10	4.7	0.5	4.4	88:12	7.2	1.1

Table 2. Changing Distribution of Education Levels and Males/Females within Those Levels – 1992 to 2012 – White Collar (All Pay Plans)

	1992				2012			
Education Level	% of Total	M:F Split	Male % Distrib.	Female % Distrib.	% of Total	M:F Split	Male % Distrib.	Female % Distrib.
< High School	1.1	36:64	0.8	1.5	0.4	34:66	0.2	0.5
High School	22.4	35:65	15.0	30.4	22.1	53:47	21.8	22.4

	1992				2012			
Education Level	% of Total	M:F Split	Male % Distrib.	Female % Distrib.	% of Total	M:F Split	Male % Distrib.	Female % Distrib.
Graduate/GED								
Occupational Training/Cert.	5.9	28:72	3.2	8.8	3.3	30:70	1.8	5.0
Some College (4 Yrs. or Less)	27.3	44:56	23.3	31.6	20.7	48:52	18.6	23.2
Bachelor Degree	24.7	66:34	31.6	17.3	29.1	58:42	31.5	26.4
Post Bachelor	7.2	73:27	10.2	4.0	5.8	58:42	6.3	5.3
Master Degree	8.0	70:30	10.8	5.0	14.7	56:44	15.4	14.0
Post Master	1.3	76:24	1.9	0.7	0.8	59:41	0.9	0.7
Doctorate	1.7	82:18	2.7	0.6	2.6	61:39	3.0	2.2
Post Doctorate	0.3	87:13	0.5	0.1	0.4	65:35	0.5	0.3

In terms of occupational category (PATCO), there has been a large reduction in Clerical employees and a large increase in Administrative employees. The percentage of Professional jobs held by females has increased from 33 percent to 45 percent. The percentage of females who hold Professional or Administrative jobs increased from 45 percent to 68 percent.

In terms of education level, the number of employees with a Bachelor Degree or higher increased from 43 percent to 53 percent. The percentage of employees holding those higher degrees who were female increased from 31 percent to 42 percent. The percentage of female employees holding those higher degrees increased from 28 percent to 49 percent.

The overall percentage of females in the Federal White Collar workforce was 48 percent in 1992 and dropped slightly to 46 percent in 2012.

B. Snapshot Data Findings

Table 3 below provides percentages capturing the male-female pay relationship at the overall level for All White Collar and for the subset GS population.[10] (Additional data is provided in Appendix 2.)

In addition to collecting snapshot data for the overall white-collar and GS populations, we also collected snapshot data for various subpopulations defined based on selected factors (e.g., age, agency, education, occupation). For example, for the Age factor, there are age ranges (e.g., 25- 34, 35-44) that define subpopulations for the factor. Appendix 3 provides a list of selected key factors and the associated subpopulations.

Table 3. Overall Summary of Gender Pay Gap for All White Collar and General Schedule Populations – as of December Snapshot in 1992, 2002, and 2012

	Female Salary Percentage*			Pay Gap**		
Year	1992	2002	2012	1992	2002	2012
White Collar (All Pay Plans)	70.0%	80.2%	87.3%	30.0%	19.8%	12.7%
General Schedule (GS-GL-GM)	70.3%	81.6%	89.2%	29.7%	18.4%	10.8%

* Female salary percentage = average female salary divided by average male salary.
** Gap represents the percentage average female salary is below average male salary.

Some of our key findings from our analysis of snapshot data are summarized below:

- Over the study years (1992-2002-2012), the pay gap has dramatically shrunk from about 30 percent to 13 percent (for All White Collar) and 11 percent (for GS only).
- The differences in the distribution of males and females across occupational categories appear to explain much of the pay gap. The more discrete the occupational groupings, the more the pay gap is explained. We used three levels of occupational groups: (1) five PATCO categories, (2) 37 groups based on combinations of PATCO code and occupational family, and (3) 350 occupational series. We computed weighted averages based on the size of the subpopulations of occupational groupings and found that those weighted averages increased as the number of occupational groups increased. For example, 97.1 percent was the population-weighted average based on the 37 occupational groups for the All White Collar population in 2012; in contrast, the raw overall gap was 87.3 percent. These data suggest that occupation explains much of the gender pay disparity.
- When we examined the female salary percentages for the 37 occupational groups in 2012, we found that the female average salary exceeded the male average salary for 15 groups (compared to 3 groups in 1992). An additional 6 groups had a female salary

percentage of at least 95 percent. (See Appendix 2 for specific details.)

- The pay gap was smaller in younger age groups. For example, in 2012, the female salary percentage was 95.1 percent for the subpopulation of All White Collar employees who are in the 25-34 age range and was 83.1 percent for those in the 55-64 age range. Pay gaps at different ages may reflect the differences in occupational distribution at those ages.

- In 2012, pay gaps were found at all education levels, almost all in the 8-10 percent range. The female salary percentages for the Education Level subpopulations were much closer to the overall raw average in 2012 than in past years; this suggests that differences in education level are explaining less of the gender pay disparity over time.

- In 2012, for supervisors and managers, the female salary percentage was 95.6 percent; however, females made up only 36 percent of supervisors and managers. Among members of the Senior Executive Service (SES), the female salary percentage was 99.2 percent; however, females made up only 33 percent of SES members.

- We examined pay gaps by grade level for the GS population and found that, in 2012, 9 out of 13 grade levels[11] showed the female average salary as higher than the male average salary, which was a significant change from earlier years. The four remaining female salary percentages were 99.9 (grades 1-3 combined), 98.7 (grade 8), 99.5 (grade 14), and 99.5 (grade 15). These data indicate that, for each GS grade, females and males had close to the same average position in range (average step position). The explanation for the difference in the overall female salary percentage (89.2 percent) and these subpopulation percentages near 100 percent is that relatively more females were found in lower grades, which may be a reflection of differences in occupational distribution. (See Appendix 4 for additional data on pay gaps by GS grade level.)

C. Regression-Decomposition Findings

OPM employed multivariate regression-decomposition analysis to determine which factors most influenced the gender pay gap. Application of decomposition methods allowed us to decompose the pay gap into an explained portion (i.e., portion attributable to the factors included in the analysis) and an unexplained portion. The explained portion measures the effect that female characteristics (i.e., percentage distribution of females across the subpopulations for each factor) have on the pay gap. The decomposition method also measures the extent to which the various factors contribute to the explained portion of the pay gap. Thus, it provides insights regarding possible causes of the pay gap. Below we present a table providing summary results of the regression-decomposition analysis, which is followed by selected observations.

Table 4. Results of Multivariate Regression and Decomposition Analysis

Population	Year	Actual Pay Gap	Estimated Pay Gap[12]	Un-explained Portion	Explained Portion	Explained Portion as % of Total Gap	% of Explained Portion Explained by Occupation
White Collar (All Pay Plans)	1992	30.0%	29.4%	4.4%	25.0%	85%	64%
	2002	19.8%	19.4%	4.4%	15.0%	77%	71%
	2012	12.7%	12.9%	3.8%	9.0%	70%	76%
General Schedule (GS-GL-GM)	1992	29.7%	29.3%	4.3%	25.0%	85%	66%
	2002	18.4%	18.5%	4.5%	14.0%	76%	73%
	2012	10.8%	11.6%	3.8%	7.8%	67%	93%

- While the total pay gap has decreased, the portion of the gap explained by included factors has decreased. The Occupation factor (37 occupational groups) had by far the largest impact on the explained portion of the pay gap. In 2012, no other factor accounted for more than 10 percent of the explained portion of the gap.
- The Education Level factor was the next most significant factor, but its effects were much less than the Occupation factor and those effects have lessened over time.

While our regression-decomposition analysis shows that some portion of the male-female pay cap is "unexplained"—that is, not explained by the factors included in our analysis—that does not mean that the unexplained gap is necessarily attributable to discrimination.

In a March 2009 report, GAO also found an unexplained portion of the male-female pay gap based on a regression-decomposition analysis similar to the one we have conducted.

GAO noted that its analysis "neither confirms nor refutes the presence of discriminatory practices" and that the unexplained gap may be due to "the inability to account for certain factors that cannot be effectively measured or for which data are not available." GAO identified the following possible theoretical explanations for the unexplained pay gap:[13]

- Discrimination,
- Imprecise measurement or reporting of data included in analysis (e.g., education level),
- Prior work experience outside the Federal Government (i.e., amount and type of experience),
- Educational major (specific field of study),
- More specific information on type of position/occupation,
- Individual priorities such as personal obligations outside of work (common data proxies are marital status and number of children), and
- Motivation and work performance.

Other possible explanations for the unexplained pay gap could be—

- Care-giving responsibilities (e.g., elder care, age of children being cared for), and
- Availability or absence of a workplace flexibility of importance to the employee (e.g., job with inflexible hours or requiring frequent travel, opportunity to telework).

It is important to also note that even if a portion of male-female pay gap is "explained" by factors included in the analysis, it does not mean that all those factors are immune from possible discriminatory influence. To the extent that the explaining factors are subject to employee or employer control, some unknown portion of the explained gap may reflect the effects of discrimination (either societal or employer-specific). Factors that are shown to have a significant statistical effect on the male-female pay gap should be closely examined to determine if there is an element of discrimination behind the differences. For example, OPM's analysis shows that the difference in occupational distribution is a key factor in explaining the male-female pay gap.

The reasons for that difference should be explored and possible strategies of reducing the difference could be implemented. If traditional societal expectations are a reason why women are not equally represented in certain higher-paying occupations, then strategies to encourage women to enter nontraditional occupational fields could be developed.

Some of the factors used in our analysis—such as age, disability status, race/ethnicity, and veterans status—are factors that could potentially generate discrimination based on the factor itself, without regard to gender. It is beyond the scope of our current analysis to examine that issue. Our analysis captures the extent to which those factors contributed to the gender pay gap.

D. Dynamic Data Findings

We collected data from OPM's Dynamics File for calendar years 1992, 2002, and 2012 for White Collar employees with respect to the use of following pay actions:

- Use of superior qualifications and special agency need pay-setting authority to set a newly hired GS employee's starting salary above the step 1 minimum rate,
- Setting of starting salaries for new hires,
- Quality step increases for GS employees with outstanding performance (i.e., a special step increase granted without regard to normal waiting periods), and
- Nontemporary promotions (excluding career-ladder promotions, reclassification promotions, and promotions resulting from the correction of a classification error).

A high-level summary of the results is provided in Appendix 5. Some of our key findings from our analysis of snapshot data are summarized below:

- *Superior qualifications and special needs pay-setting actions* (hereafter, referred to as "superior qualifications actions") were used more frequently (on a percentage basis) for males than females in all 3 years.
  - In 2012, the percentage of male new hires receiving these actions was 12.6 percent, while the corresponding percentage of female new hires was 8.3 percent. In 2012, about 35 percent of all such actions were used for females and 65 percent for males. However, 45 percent of new hires were female.

o Closer analysis reveals that superior qualification actions are more heavily used in certain occupational categories that are more male-dominated. In 2012, about 44 percent of superior qualification actions occurred in 3 out of 37 occupational categories—08xx-Professional (mainly engineers), 22xx-Administration (information technology), and Xxxx-Professional (other Professional)—which covered only 12 percent of the total GS workforce. During calendar year 2012, the percentage of new hires in those occupations who were female was 19 percent, 20 percent, and 33 percent, respectively. Thus, these male-dominated occupational categories had a disproportionate effect on the usage rates for superior qualifications actions.

• *Starting salaries were lower for females than males, on average, in all 3 years.*

o The overall pay gap in starting salaries for new hires was about 10-11 percent in 2012, just slightly below the overall pay gap for on-board White Collar employees.

o The difference between the starting salary pay gap and the on-board employee pay gap has gotten smaller over time; that difference was 13-14 percent in 1992 and 1-2 percent in 2012. These statistics confirm that the composition of the workforce is changing over time as females enter the workforce with higher average starting salaries.

o When we analyzed White Collar starting salaries for the 37 more-specific occupational categories in 2012, we found that female starting salaries exceeded male starting salaries for 14 categories and were within 5 percent of male starting salaries for another 12 categories. Only 4 categories had pay gaps of more than 10 percent (no more than 12 percent). Differences in occupational distribution between males and females appear to explain much of the overall starting salary pay gap of 10.7 percent.

o When we examined White Collar starting salaries by education levels, we found some shifts in pay gaps at the various levels in both directions between 1992 and 2012. We computed a population-weighted average pay gap (based on the percentage of new hires in each education level subpopulation) and found that gap was stable over the 3 years (about 89.4-89.5 percent). In 2012, the overall raw pay gap of 10.7 percent was close to the population-weighted average pay gap of 10.5 percent. This suggests that factors other than education level were behind the starting salary pay gap.

o When we examined GS starting salaries by GS grade level, we found that male and female average starting salaries were quite close in all three years (1992, 2002, 2012). While females appear to be treated equally at the same grade level, females tend to be employed at lower grades on average; thus, there was an overall pay gap, which, as noted above, appears to be largely attributable to differences in occupational distribution, which in turn affects grade distribution.

- *Quality step increases* (QSIs) were awarded more frequently (on a percentage basis) to females than males in all 3 years.

o In 2012, the percentage of GS females receiving a QSI was 3.53, while the corresponding male percentage was 3.11. In 2012, 50.7 percent of QSIs were awarded to females, while they made up only 47.5 percent of the GS workforce. In 2012, the female QSI advantage applied in each PATCO occupational category.

o When we examined QSI usage rates for the 37 more-specific occupational categories in 2012, we found that the female QSI usage rate exceeded the male rate for 31 of 37 categories. Thus, differences in occupational distribution between males and females did not seem to explain the female advantage in QSI usage rates.

o In 2012, the female QSI usage rate exceeded the male rate at all 10 educational levels, except the level for Occupational Training/Certificate.

o In 2012, the female QSI usage rate exceeded the male rate at all GS grade levels 2-15, except for the small-population GS-8 grade.

o When we examined the male/female QSI usage rates by agency in 2012, we found some agencies where the male usage rate was higher than the female rate.

- *Promotions* were received more frequently (on a percentage basis) by females than males in all 3 years.

o For the White Collar population in 2012, the overall promotion rate was 3.94 percent for females and 3.38 percent for males. Females received 50.1 percent of promotions even though they made up just 46.3 percent of the total White Collar workforce.

o When we examined White Collar promotion rates for the 37 more-specific occupational categories in 2012, we found that the female promotion rate exceeded the male rate for 27 of 37 categories. The overall average promotion rate was affected by the promotion rate for each occupational category and the mix of males and females in each category.

o   In 2012, the White Collar female promotion rate exceeded the male rate at all 10 educational levels, except the level for Occupational Training/Certificate.

V. GOVERNMENTWIDE STRATEGY

The President's May 10, 2013, memorandum directed the Director of OPM to submit to the President a Governmentwide strategy to address any gender pay gap in the Federal workforce.

Based on our data analysis and the information reported to OPM by agencies, OPM recommends the following Governmentwide strategy for each of the three issue areas covered by the President's memorandum:

A. Analysis of Whether Changes to the General Schedule Classification System Would Assist in Addressing Any Gender Pay Gap

Recommendation: OPM will work with agencies to review their internal classification policies and application of GS classification system in compliance with the principle of equal pay for substantially equal work.

The classification standards program for GS positions was established by the Classification Act of 1949, and has been codified in chapter 51 of title 5, United States Code.

The statute establishes the principle of providing equal pay for substantially equal work. After a comprehensive review of agency reports, there were no indicators that changes to the GS classification system would assist in addressing any gender pay gap. There was no evidence provided by agencies that the law (i.e., 5 U.S.C. chapter 51), regulations (i.e., 5 CFR part 511), and OPM's policies and standards on GS classification may be affecting gender pay equality.

In fact, adherence to the principle of equal pay for equal work is evident based on the agency data collected and reviewed for this study. Although the

GS classification system was not indicated as having an effect on gender pay equality, future agency studies may focus on the *application* of the GS classification system.

Additionally, OPM will assist agencies, in exercising their delegated classification authority, in collecting metrics and other relevant agency data to examine classification practices based on a variety of factors, including gender analysis by occupation.

For example, data collected in this study indicate pay gaps in some traditionally non-female occupations, i.e., occupations where female representation is below 25 percent particularly in certain science, engineering, and related "technical" occupations. Other data indicate pay gaps in some predominantly female occupations (where women representation is 50-60 percent or more of the occupation). (See Appendix 3.) OPM will explore future agency studies of such occupations in terms of grade patterns by gender so that agencies can better assess the effective application of the GS classification system.

In support, OPM will work with agencies to review their application of classification policies and identify their need for guidance and/or training to support human resources (HR) professionals in the application of the GS classification system, and provide tools and guidance on key classification policy issues.

OPM currently hosts quarterly Classification Policy Forum with agency classification leads. OPM will use this forum to discuss and identify possible gender pay gap issues as they pertain to classification practices. We will also use the forum may to champion agency best practices regarding gender pay equality, and to provide support to agencies to promote internal agency partnerships that include their HR, Equal Employment Opportunity and Diversity and Inclusion Offices with the common goal of gender pay equality.

B. Proposed Guidance to Agencies to Promote Greater Transparency Regarding Starting Salaries

Recommendation 1: OPM will work with agencies to ensure GS equivalent-level salary tables or rate ranges are made available to job candidates.

One component to help ensure transparent starting salaries is to make pay tables or rate ranges for positions readily available to job candidates.

OPM posts the GS and other Governmentwide pay tables that OPM administers on its public website.[14] As stated previously, the GS system covers the majority of the Federal workforce.

Another component to help ensure transparency in starting salaries is to provide salary information for a vacant position in a job announcement. Agencies are required by law and regulation to post starting pay on competitive service job announcements. Under 5 U.S.C. 3330, OPM must establish and keep current a comprehensive list of all announcements of vacant positions in the competitive service within each agency that are to be filled by appointment for more than 1 year and for which applications are being (or will soon be) accepted from outside the agency's work force. OPM's regulations implementing this law for competitive service positions are in 5 CFR 330.104.

Regarding salary, they state that the vacancy must contain the starting pay. OPM maintains USAJOBS (*www.usajobs.gov*) as a web-based job board to meet its legal obligation. Any position listed must include a brief description of the position, including its title, tenure, location, and rate of pay. Often agencies post the rate range for the position. For example, the agency would post the step 1 rate (the minimum rate) and the step 10 rate (maximum rate) for a GS grade including any locality payment or special rate supplement for the position.

In the gender pay equality information request, OPM asked agencies whether pay tables or rate ranges for their GS equivalent-level employees are available to the public. Agencies provided mixed responses. Some agencies mentioned that the non-GS rate ranges were posted on job announcements. Eight agencies responded that their non-GS pay tables or rate ranges are available to the public on their websites. Four agencies mentioned that they use a pay system that is identical to the GS system, which is available on OPM's website. Five agencies stated that some of their GS equivalent-level pay tables or rate ranges are available to the public and some are not. Six agencies indicated that none of their equivalent-level pay tables or rate ranges are available to the public.

Agencies shared a variety of reasons why they do not provide their non-GS pay tables or rate ranges to the public including the agency being new, there being no legal requirement to do so, or administrative difficulties because there are too many pay tables.

OPM will work with agencies with GS equivalent-level pay systems to post salary tables or rate ranges on their public websites. Ensuring agencies post such information on their respective websites would provide transparency regarding non-GS pay rates for all job candidates. In addition, such information should be updated as soon as there are increases or other changes to their pay tables or rate ranges and include agency contact information about the pay system for all job applicants.

Recommendation 2: OPM will explore ways to ensure pay-setting options and other salary information is made readily available to job candidates.

Ensuring that all job applicants understand agency pay-setting options and have other salary information available promotes starting salary transparency. A new GS employee is usually hired at step 1 of the applicable GS grade. However, in special circumstances, agencies may authorize a higher step rate for a newly-appointed Federal employee based on a special need of the agency or superior qualifications of the prospective employee. (Newly-appointed includes employees who are reappointed after at least a 90-day break in service.) Current Federal employees who move to a GS position and are not considered newly appointed may have pay set above step 1 based only on a previous Federal civilian rate of pay (i.e., maximum payable rate rule) under the gaining agency's policies.

OPM has fact sheets on the superior qualifications and special needs pay setting authority and the maximum payable rate rule that an agency may use to set an employee's starting salary on its public website.[15] OPM also has a fact sheet on GS classification and pay.[16] However, job applicants may not know to look for the fact sheets.

Generally, most agencies reported that they do not provide all applicants information on the pay-setting flexibilities the agency uses and, of those that provide information, there is no consistent approach. A few agencies or components within agencies reported making their use of payflexibilities public on vacancy announcements, the agency's website, or at job fairs. Several agencies stated that they provide information upon request. Agencies may discuss pay flexibilities with candidates during the interview process, when the candidate is tentatively selected, or if the candidate declines the position.

OPM will explore whether to provide links to its fact sheets and other information on starting salaries for GS positions on USAJOBS or on OPM's public website.

OPM also will work with agencies to ensure that information regarding the pay flexibilities that they use and other salary information is also made available to all job candidates for GS and non-GS pay systems.

If the information is accessible, it increases the likelihood that all job candidates will ask about the pay flexibilities and be better able to discuss them with the agency during the hiring process.

C. Recommendations for Additional Administrative or Legislative Actions or Studies

Recommendation 1: OPM will work with agencies to clarify the range of GS pay-setting flexibility and share best practices on setting starting salaries in gender-neutral ways.

The GS pay system is designed with standardized rules and criteria for setting pay for employees entering Federal service for the first time, returning to Federal employment, and upon promotion and other position changes within the Federal Government. These standardized rules help to promote equitable treatment among employees. Where there is pay-setting flexibility, agencies must ensure such flexibilities are exercised in gender-neutral ways so as not to disadvantage any individual, such as those returning to the workplace after a career break.

OPM's regulations in 5 CFR part 531, subpart B, provide criteria for using the superior qualifications and special needs pay-setting authority for GS positions.

After an agency has determined that a candidate has superior qualifications or the agency has a special need for the candidate's services, the agency determines the step at which to set the employee's rate of basic pay. The regulations state that an agency may consider one or more of nine listed factors (including a candidate's existing pay, recent salary history, or salary in a competing job offer), or other relevant factors when making this determination.

Most agencies with GS employees reported using the superior qualifications and special needs pay-setting authority in fiscal year (FY) 2012 and have written policies on the authority. Agency reports provide a wide variety of examples of approval requirements, criteria, or limitations that they have established in addition to those required by OPM's regulations. These include an approval level that is higher than what is required by the regulations, limiting how high pay can be set above a candidate's existing pay, stating what factors must be considered or what additional factors may be considered when setting pay, and limiting use of the authority to higher-level positions or certain occupations.

While OPM's regulations provide agencies the discretion to consider a candidate's existing salary when setting pay under this authority, 14 agencies stated that they require the use of the candidate's existing salary or that the existing salary must be considered. This could potentially adversely affect a candidate who is returning to the workplace after having taken extended time off from his or her career.

Some agencies shared examples of how they set pay under the superior qualifications and special needs pay-setting authority using well-defined approval criteria. They set pay at a predetermined step or pay rate for job candidates with similar education or experience who are filling a group or category of similar positions.

For example, one agency component sets pay at a certain grade and step based on the type of degree the candidate holds and the candidate also must have a specified class rank or grade point average and have attended an accredited school. Another agency component applies a "blind practice method" where the HR office sets pay rather than the hiring official to eliminate pay disparities. The HR office assesses the graduation year from school, type and length of relevant experience, and the current salary of the candidate (as a last consideration).

The criteria for using the maximum payable rate (MPR) rule for GS positions also is in 5 CFR part 531, subpart B. Most agencies reported using this rule in FY 2012. Over half of the agencies with GS employees have written policies, and about half of those policies are more specific than the regulations.

Most agency or component policies do not address how recent the employee's highest previous rate (HPR) must be to be used in applying the MPR rule. One agency commented that the MPR rule helps minimize any negative impact that may occur for employees who have extended breaks in service. (Under this rule, an agency compares the employee's HPR to the applicable rate range in effect when the employee earned his or her HPR to find the MPR and then brings the step forward to the current applicable rate range.)

One agency uses a compensation panel to recommend pay for one group of its GS equivalent-level employees and boards to recommend pay for its other GS equivalent-level employees.

The panel and boards include employees in the occupation for which pay is being set. They have specific criteria to consider when setting pay, such as setting pay based on the number of years of service in the occupation in the agency and supervisory or managerial level.

OPM will work with agencies to determine where additional guidance may be needed on the superior qualifications and special needs pay-setting authority to clarify the factors that may be used to set pay. While agency policies may place more restrictions on pay setting than OPM's regulations, we will provide guidance to agencies to make sure they consider the complete picture of the candidate and the situation rather than placing too much emphasis on a candidate's existing pay.

OPM also will work with agencies to identify and share best practices with agencies on setting starting salaries in gender-neutral ways. This could include setting pay based on specific criteria for certain occupations and using compensation panels that do not include hiring managers to recommend the use of pay flexibilities. Agencies may want to consider the diversity of the panel members when establishing a panel.

Recommendation 2: OPM will develop guidance for agencies to conduct their own gender data analyses, review their starting salary trends and use of pay-setting flexibilities, and review their promotion data to determine if gender equity issues are apparent so that they can develop approaches to address any issues.

Most agencies reported that they do not review their use of pay-setting flexibilities on a periodic basis to examine the gender distribution of employees for which the authorities are used. Most reports also did not indicate that agencies perform other types of pay or promotion data analyses by gender on a routine basis. The few agencies or components within agencies that reported conducting such reviews have different methods. One agency and an agency component with GS equivalent-level pay systems compare the average salaries of men and women by grade level. Another agency with a GS equivalent-level pay system conducted a statistical analysis to compare salaries.

Components at two agencies with GS employees periodically review their use of pay-setting flexibilities. One focuses on tracking information on use of the superior qualifications and special needs pay-setting authority and then using the information to inform future determinations regarding the use of the authority.

OPM (or an interagency workgroup, including OPM) will develop guidance for agencies on how they can conduct data analyses similar to those that OPM conducted for the purposes of this strategy. This could include reviewing starting salary trends, the use of pay-setting flexibilities, and promotion data to determine if there are any differences when examining the gender of employees and the reasons for those differences. Agencies could then develop strategies to address any differences that they find.

Recommendation 3: OPM will explore the need to conduct additional Governmentwide statistical analyses to obtain a better understanding of gender pay trends for specific categories of employees not covered by OPM's initial data review.

In performing data analysis to support this report, we focused primarily on white-collar employees. We performed regression-decomposition analysis only for the total white-collar population. We believe additional regression-decomposition analyses may be useful.

For example, we could perform a regression-decomposition analysis for blue-collar employees. In addition, we could perform regression-decomposition analyses for specific subpopulations within the white-collar workforce, such as occupational groups with the largest pay gaps or newly hired employees. We will also explore presenting certain gender-based snapshot data in two layers, such as showing data by (1) occupational category and (2) education level.

Recommendation 4: OPM will work with agencies to share best practices and develop recruitment and outreach strategies for growing female populations in occupations where they are underrepresented, e.g., STEM, nontraditional, and supervisory and managerial jobs.

As previously stated, the differences in the distribution of males and females across occupational categories appear to explain much of the pay gap. Therefore, OPM will work with agencies to share best practices and develop recruitment and outreach strategies for growing female populations in occupations where they are underrepresented, such as STEM and other nontraditional jobs, and supervisory and managerial jobs, as part of an overall recruitment plan.

Eight reporting agencies use targeted outreach to attract more women as prospective employees. Two agencies maintain relationships with colleges and universities to promote career opportunities. One agency component started a print campaign targeting national publications geared towards female business professionals in certain markets and increased their social media presence, and made it a point to target women through women specific conferences and symposiums. One agency portrays women in higher-paying occupations in print and online recruitment materials. Another agency sponsors and participates in the Society of Women Engineers annual conference to recruit women for STEM occupations.

A different agency conducts activities with particular constituent communities, including those with primary professional women membership.

One agency reported that a component created a division-wide recruitment team to create a strategic approach to recruiting and selecting future employees, and eliminate any barriers resulting in inequality of employment. The team ensures that all markets, including those that have a majority male representation, are considered when recruiting for qualified candidates to fill the division's mission-critical occupations. Another agency also utilizes recruitment plans for high-level positions.

Each recruitment plan is carefully researched to find websites for qualified women and minorities, as part of the overall recruitment plan. The agency has found this to be a low-cost and successful way to reach diverse populations.

OPM will continue to provide training for agency HR professionals, agency hiring managers, and Special Programs Coordinators on how to conduct strategic recruitment for mission-critical occupations and hard-to-find skills, including STEM. In FY 2013, OPM trained 1,100 Federal employees in 33 individual two-day sessions.

OPM plans to promote agency "best practices" in our newly created Recruiting Policy suite on HR University.[17] Information on recruiting strategies and effective outreach practices to attract and recruit a diverse workforce will be available to agencies.

OPM is creating video tutorials for job seekers available on USAJOBS' YouTube to educate them on the Federal hiring process and hiring programs such as Pathways Programs.[18] Agencies can post OPM-developed outreach materials and videos on their agency websites.

OPM will partner with minority and professional organizations to educate women job seekers on how to find and apply for Federal jobs, the Federal hiring process, Federal resume writing, and career opportunities in the Federal Government (including the Presidential Management Fellows Program/STEM track). In addition, OPM will continue to partner with the Federal Chief Information Officers Council to expand and enhance the Federal Job Shadow Day Governmentwide and nationwide with an emphasis on women and minorities in STEM.

OPM will continue to work with the National Initiative for Cybersecurity Education (NICE) to promote Federal careers, education, and training opportunities to women and minorities.

OPM will continue to work with partners from the private and public sector to increase awareness of Federal STEM occupations by enhancing the Federal presence at Science and Engineering Festivals, Cybersecurity Competitions, etc. OPM will expand social media outreach to include groups and resources directed to women to reach broader, targeted audiences and to raise awareness of agencies' mission and career opportunities.

OPM will seek out collaborative recruiting relationships with colleges and universities, technical and trade schools, professional associations, and student organizations to improve outreach effectiveness and to broaden access to employment opportunities for women, as part of an overall outreach strategy.

Recommendation 5: OPM will work with agencies to share best practices and develop guidance for when to consider work schedule changes to part-time.

Most agencies reported they do not have specific policies in place for establishing part-time positions outside of policies required by the Part-Time Career Act, which included consideration of job-sharing opportunities. A few of the larger agencies have overarching policies that require consideration of organizational needs but ultimately leave the decision to manager discretion. Some smaller agencies establish positions only as full-time but will consider individual employee requests to switch to part-time. Almost all reporting agencies consider employee requests to switch to a part-time work schedule on a case-by-case basis.

Decisions are left to the manager/supervisor without specific agency-wide criteria to consider. However, most agencies reported that managers consider factors such as the effect on the organization, on the workload, and on the workforce when deciding whether to approve the request. A few agencies also consider work/life balance and whether disapproval will cause the employee to resign.

All agencies reported part-time promotion opportunities are advertised and part-time employees are considered and evaluated for promotion on the same basis as full-time opportunities and employees.

Positions with part-time work schedules are a small percentage of all work schedules (3 percent) with females totaling 61 percent of those schedules.[19] The majority of part-time work schedules are in grades below the GS-12 level. As mentioned above, every reporting agency considers organizational workload and needs when deciding employee requests for part-time work schedules; however, few agencies have uniform criteria in place.

OPM will explore whether the lack of part-time schedules at higher levels is based on the lack of or inconsistent criteria used in approving requests. OPM will also work with agencies to share best practices and develop general criteria or guidance to aid with agency consistency and transparency.

OPM also will explore with agencies the feasibility of establishing more positions as part-time job-sharing positions— i.e., two or more part-time employees performing the work of one full-time position, to increase the number of promotional opportunities for part-time employees, the majority of whom are female. Although agencies reported that part-time employees are considered for promotions on the same basis as full-time employees, additional study is needed to determine the percentage of those employees who must change to a full-time schedule if selected. Depending on the basis for the part-time schedule, part-time employees may be reluctant to accept the higher graded position if doing so would require changing to a full-time schedule. Increasing job-sharing opportunities may provide additional promotion opportunities for females on part-time schedules.

VI. APPENDICES

1. Summary of Subpopulation Percentages, Male-Female Split, and Male/Female Distributions by Subpopulation
2. Overall Summary of Snapshot Data by Year—White-Collar (All Pay Plans) and General Schedule Total Populations
3. Summary of Key Snapshot Data by Subpopulations by Year
4. Snapshot Data by General Schedule Grade Level
5. Summary of Dynamic Data Findings

APPENDIX 1.

Summary of Subpopulation Percentages, Male-Female Split, and Male/Female Distributions by Subpopulation

White Collar (All Pay Plans)
Nonseasonal full-time permanent employees in pay status in the Executive Branch

	Dec. 1992				Dec. 2002				Dec. 2012			
	% of Total Population	M:F % Split	Male % Distribution	Female % Distribution	% of Total Population	M:F % Split	Male % Distribution	Female % Distribution	% of Total Population	M:F % Split	Male % Distribution	Female % Distribution
Total Population	100.00	52 :48	100.00	100.00	100.00	52 :48	100.00	100.00	100.00	54 :46	100.00	100.00

Factors: Subpopulations

Age category (years)

	% of Total Population	M:F % Split	Male % Distribution	Female % Distribution	% of Total Population	M:F % Split	Male % Distribution	Female % Distribution	% of Total Population	M:F % Split	Male % Distribution	Female % Distribution
<25	2.60	31 :69	1.62	3.95	1.67	50 :50	1.60	1.75	1.05	51 :49	1.00	1.11
25-34	20.39	45 :55	17.65	23.32	12.09	52 :48	12.01	12.19	16.58	54 :46	16.70	16.34
35-44	32.84	49 :51	31.37	34.41	27.52	50 :50	26.41	28.74	22.30	54 :46	22.60	22.15
45-54	30.11	58 :42	33.60	26.37	29.15	52 :49	27.58	29.70	33.42	54 :46	23.34	23.52
55-64	12.45	59 :41	14.14	10.64	18.65	57 :43	20.28	16.87	22.03	52 :48	22.28	23.60
65+	1.59	55 :45	1.62	1.42	1.92	59 :41	2.15	1.67	3.63	60 :41	4.01	3.19

Education level

Below High School	1.14	36 :64	0.80	1.50	0.71	32 :68	0.44	1.01	0.35	34 :66	0.22	0.50
High School Graduate Or Equivalency (GED)	22.44	35 :65	15.00	30.39	24.18	43 :57	19.91	28.87	22.12	53 :47	21.84	22.44
Occupational Training/Certificate Or Equivalency	5.92	28 :72	3.21	8.81	4.20	29 :71	2.35	6.23	3.32	30 :70	1.84	5.04
Some College (4 Years Or Less)	27.33	44 :56	23.33	31.61	24.85	45 :55	21.36	28.90	20.74	48 :52	18.62	23.20
Bachelor Degree	24.67	66 :34	31.56	17.31	26.30	62 :38	31.08	21.05	29.13	58 :42	31.48	26.39
Post Bachelor	7.24	73 :27	10.23	4.04	6.38	66 :34	8.07	4.51	5.84	58 :42	6.32	5.28
Master Degree	7.97	70 :30	10.76	4.98	9.94	64 :36	12.09	7.58	14.72	56 :44	15.38	13.96
Post Master	1.31	76 :24	1.93	0.65	0.97	70 :30	1.30	0.61	0.79	59 :41	0.88	0.70
Doctorate Degree	1.68	82 :18	2.67	0.63	2.04	74 :26	2.90	1.10	2.82	61 :39	2.99	2.19
Post Doctorate	0.30	87 :13	0.51	0.08	0.33	79 :21	0.51	0.15	0.38	65 :35	0.48	0.29

Length of service category (years)

<5	16.95	43 :57	14.00	20.10	16.17	54 :46	16.64	15.66	26.96	56 :44	28.13	25.60
5-9	20.82	47 :53	18.80	22.88	10.38	56 :44	11.06	9.83	19.53	57 :43	20.64	18.24
10-14	17.94	48 :52	16.58	19.42	16.77	49 :51	15.72	17.92	14.74	57 :43	15.81	13.73
15-19	16.13	51 :49	16.02	16.25	18.46	49 :51	17.37	19.67	7.98	58 :44	8.27	7.65
20-24	13.12	60 :40	15.18	10.94	15.19	49 :51	14.15	16.33	11.04	49 :51	10.08	12.18
25-29	9.05	62 :38	10.81	7.17	12.50	53 :47	12.74	12.24	10.20	48 :52	9.10	11.49
30-34	4.21	74 :26	6.00	2.30	7.47	62 :38	8.80	8.03	5.95	46 :54	5.03	7.01
35+	1.77	74 :26	2.54	0.95	3.05	61 :39	3.53	2.53	3.60	47 :53	3.17	4.11

Occupational Category #1 (PATCO)

A-Administrative	32.70	60 :40	38.07	26.96	39.96	55 :45	42.18	37.52	43.61	57 :43	46.35	40.42
C-Clerical	15.75	14 :86	4.21	28.09	7.49	18 :82	2.57	12.90	5.31	31 :69	3.06	7.94
O-Other White Collar	2.68	90 :10	4.68	0.54	3.58	89 :11	6.07	0.81	4.38	88 :12	7.20	1.10
P-Professional	28.55	67 :33	34.38	18.17	28.21	62 :38	30.94	21.01	27.98	55 :45	28.82	27.23
T-Technical	22.32	43 :57	18.66	26.24	22.78	42 :58	18.24	27.76	18.72	42 :58	14.77	23.32

Occupational Category #2 (PATCO and Job Family)

	Dec. 1992				Dec. 2002				Dec. 2012			
	% of Total Population	M:F % Split	Male % Distribution	Female % Distribution	% of Total Population	M:F % Split	Male % Distribution	Female % Distribution	% of Total Population	M:F % Split	Male % Distribution	Female % Distribution
00xx-A Miscellaneous Occupations (Admin)	1.45	71:29	2.00	0.87	1.84	67:33	2.34	1.29	1.83	68:32	2.30	1.29
00xx-O Miscellaneous Occupations (Other)	2.20	93:7	3.96	0.31	2.63	91:9	4.56	0.51	2.80	90:10	4.70	0.59
01xx-A Social Science, Psychology, and Welfare (Admin)	1.94	43:57	1.61	2.28	2.62	39:61	1.93	3.37	2.66	42:58	2.05	3.36
01xx-P Social Science, Psychology, and Welfare (Prof)	1.55	64:36	1.92	1.15	1.80	56:44	1.94	1.65	2.22	42:58	1.74	2.78
02xx-A Personnel Mgmt & Industrial Relations (Admin)	1.93	39:61	1.46	2.42	1.89	30:70	1.08	2.78	1.80	30:70	1.01	2.72
03xx-A General Admin, Clerical, & Office Svcs (Admin)	7.78	53:47	7.91	7.58	9.88	45:55	8.43	11.44	12.24	48:52	10.99	13.70
03xx-C General Admin, Clerical, & Office Svcs (Clerical)	10.00	11:89	2.39	10.99	5.34	15:85	1.53	9.52	2.41	21:79	0.94	4.11
03xx-T General Admin, Clerical, & Office Svcs (Tech)	3.56	25:75	1.73	5.52	3.73	21:79	1.49	6.19	2.90	26:74	1.39	4.65
04xx-P Natural Resources Mgmt & Bio Sci Group (Prof)	2.32	80:20	3.59	0.95	2.48	72:28	3.40	1.42	2.23	65:35	2.67	1.71
05xx-A Accounting and Budget (Admin)	1.88	45:55	1.60	2.13	2.53	37:63	1.77	3.37	2.81	37:63	1.95	3.82
05xx-P Accounting and Budget (Prof)	2.87	64:36	3.55	2.15	2.54	56:44	2.70	2.36	2.27	47:53	2.00	2.59
05xx-T Accounting and Budget (Tech)	3.28	20:80	1.29	5.41	2.13	21:79	0.85	3.53	1.57	26:74	0.75	2.51
06xx-C Medical, Hospital, Dental & Pub Health (Clerical)	0.75	19:81	0.27	1.25	0.61	21:79	0.24	1.01	1.15	28:72	0.59	1.80

Occupation											
06xx-T Medical, Hospital, Dental & Pub Health (Tech)	3.57	33:67	2.28	4.06	3.39	30:70	1.95	4.98	4.18	29:71	2.22	8.46
08xx-P Engineering And Architecture (Prof)	7.32	91:9	12.87	1.40	6.38	88:12	10.76	1.57	6.07	84:16	8.52	2.05
08xx-T Engineering and Architecture (Tech)	3.12	92:8	5.57	0.50	2.12	91:9	3.71	0.38	1.55	92:8	2.65	0.28
09xx-A Legal and Kindred (Admin)	1.20	42:58	0.97	1.45	1.50	35:65	0.99	2.05	1.76	38:62	1.23	2.38
09xx-P Legal and Kindred (Prof)	1.59	67:33	2.07	1.08	1.91	61:39	2.24	1.55	2.07	55:45	2.12	2.02
09xx-T Legal and Kindred (Tech)	1.50	22:78	0.83	2.43	2.52	22:78	1.04	4.14	2.03	27:73	1.01	3.21
11xx-A Business and Industry (Admin)	2.59	61:39	3.05	2.09	2.88	54:46	2.99	2.76	2.52	52:48	2.43	2.62
11xx-P Business and Industry (Prof)	2.02	44:56	1.70	2.36	1.90	39:61	1.43	2.43	2.16	44:56	1.75	2.64
11xx-T Business and Industry (Tech)	1.42	37:63	1.03	1.83	1.15	35:65	0.77	1.57	0.93	44:56	0.78	1.12
13xx-P Physical Sciences (Prof)	2.16	83:17	3.47	0.75	1.85	79:21	2.79	0.82	1.50	73:27	2.03	0.87
15xx-P Mathematics and Statistics (Prof)	0.83	72:28	1.16	0.48	0.91	68:32	1.17	0.61	0.98	67:33	1.23	0.69
18xx-AO Investigation (A+1898O & 1899O) (include occs 1898 and 1899 under code O)	4.11	82:18	6.50	1.55	6.28	80:20	9.55	2.65	8.00	80:20	11.97	3.38
18xx-T Investigation (Tech)	0.77	67:33	1.00	0.53	1.08	50:50	1.02	1.11	2.22	56:44	2.32	2.09
21xx-A Transportation (Admin)	2.05	84:16	3.32	0.70	2.65	84:16	4.23	0.91	2.13	83:17	3.27	0.79
2181-2183-T Transportation (T - Pilot, Navigator)	0.18	99:1	0.35	0.00	0.21	98:2	0.40	0.01	0.19	98:2	0.35	0.01
21xx-T* Transportation (all other 21xxT)	0.23	57:43	0.26	0.20	0.32	49:51	0.30	0.34	0.25	60:40	0.27	0.22
22xx-A Information Technology (Admin)	3.45	61:39	4.10	2.75	4.60	60:40	5.30	3.83	4.79	69:31	8.17	3.19
Xxxxx-P All other occupations with P code	1.34	52:48	1.34	1.33	1.26	56:44	1.34	1.18	1.38	59:41	1.53	1.21
Xxxxx-A All other occupations with A code	4.65	67:33	8.05	3.15	3.90	63:37	4.88	3.04	4.17	65:35	5.05	3.14
Xxxxx-T All other occupations with T code	4.70	50:50	4.55	4.85	6.14	57:43	6.72	5.52	2.91	56:44	3.03	2.76
Xxxxx-C All other occupations with C code	4.11	19:81	1.54	6.85	1.55	27:73	0.80	2.38	1.76	47:53	1.53	2.02

Pay system

GS, GL, & GM combined	92.85	52 : 48	93.08	92.59	83.32	50 : 50	80.11	86.84	80.70	53 : 47	79.00	82.67
Senior Executive Service	0.54	67 : 13	0.91	0.14	0.49	74 : 26	0.70	0.28	0.47	67 : 33	0.59	0.34
VA Nurse	2.19	14 : 86	0.58	3.90	2.36	17 : 83	0.78	4.11	3.23	19 : 81	1.11	5.69
Other	4.42	63 : 37	5.41	3.37	13.83	70 : 30	18.41	8.79	15.60	67 : 33	19.30	11.29

Race/Ethnicity

American Indian/Alaskan Native	1.58	40 : 60	1.23	1.95	1.84	39 : 61	1.38	2.34	1.95	38 : 62	1.17	2.21
Asian & Native Hawaiian/Pacific Islander	2.84	53 : 47	2.88	2.78	3.95	52 : 48	3.92	3.99	5.81	52 : 48	5.64	0.00
Black/African American	16.28	30 : 70	9.50	23.53	17.24	32 : 68	10.71	24.62	17.96	37 : 63	12.23	24.68
Hispanic/Latino	5.09	52 : 48	5.11	5.08	6.90	55 : 45	7.20	6.58	8.23	57 : 43	8.70	7.68
White	73.05	57 : 43	80.06	66.13	69.32	57 : 43	76.11	61.87	65.33	59 : 41	71.30	58.38
Other	0.56	54 : 46	0.59	0.53	0.64	55 : 45	0.67	0.60	1.01	52 : 48	0.98	1.05

Supervisory status

Manager/Supervisor	14.87	71 : 29	20.48	8.87	12.35	67 : 33	15.78	8.60	13.75	64 : 36	16.37	10.71
Non-Manager/Supervisor	85.13	48 : 52	79.52	91.13	87.65	50 : 50	84.22	91.40	86.25	52 : 48	83.63	89.29

Note: OPM collected similar data on other factors--agency, bargaining unit status, disability status, duty station, law enforcement officer status, and veteran status--which are not presented in this report for sake of brevity.

APPENDIX 2.

Overall Summary of Snapshot Data by Year --White-Collar (All Pay Plans) and General Schedule Total Populations

A. White-Collar Employees (All Pay Plans)
Nonseasonal Full-Time Permanent Employees in Pay Status in the Executive Branch

Snapshot Date	Total Empl	% of Total Pop	# Male Empl	# Female Empl	% Female	Avg Sal	Male Avg Sal	Female Avg Sal	Female/ Male Sal %	Pay Gap
Dec. 1992	1,529,311	100.0%	790,194	739,117	48.3%	$37,980	$44,412	$31,104	70.0%	30.0%
Dec. 2002	1,395,007	100.0%	729,869	665,138	47.7%	$58,844	$64,965	$52,128	80.2%	19.8%
Dec. 2012	1,669,640	100.0%	897,880	771,760	46.2%	$81,363	$86,432	$75,467	87.3%	12.7%

B. General Schedule (GS-GL-GM)
Nonseasonal Full-Time Permanent Employees in Pay Status in the Executive Branch

Snapshot Date	Total Empl	% of White-Collar Pop	# Male Empl	# Female Empl	% Female	Avg Sal	Male Avg Sal	Female Avg Sal	Female/ Male Sal %	Pay Gap
Dec. 1992	1,419,976	92.9%	735,619	684,357	48.2%	$36,667	$42,793	$30,082	70.3%	29.7%
Dec. 2002	1,162,327	83.3%	584,713	577,614	49.7%	$55,994	$61,614	$50,306	81.6%	18.4%
Dec. 2012	1,347,362	80.7%	709,314	638,048	47.4%	$76,432	$80,569	$71,833	89.2%	10.8%

APPENDIX 3.

Summary of Key Snapshot Data by Subpopulations by Year

White-Collar Employees (All Pay Plans)

Nonseasonal Full-Time Permanent Employees in Pay Status in the Executive Branch

	Dec. 1992			Dec. 2002			Dec. 2012		
	% of Total Pop	% Female	Female/ Male Sal %	% of Total Pop	% Female	Female/ Male Sal %	% of Total Pop	% Female	Female/ Male Sal %
Total population	100.0	48.3	70.0	100.0	47.7	80.2	100.0	46.2	87.3
Factors:									
Subpopulations:									
Age									
<25	2.7	69.0	90.4	1.7	50.0	94.5	1.1	48.7	92.1
25-34	20.4	55.3	77.6	12.1	48.0	93.5	16.6	45.5	95.1
35-44	32.8	50.6	75.9	27.5	49.8	80.9	22.4	45.7	91.5
45-54	30.1	42.3	68.7	38.1	48.5	81.0	33.4	46.4	86.2
55-64	12.4	41.3	63.9	18.7	43.1	74.7	22.9	47.8	83.1
65+	1.5	44.9	57.9	1.9	41.4	66.4	3.6	40.6	75.4
Population-weighted average			*72.7*			*81.3*			*87.8*
Agency									
Agriculture	6.0	40.6	71.4	6.0	43.5	83.3	4.5	45.1	92.7
Defense	39.7	45.6	69.2	33.0	43.3	78.0	33.7	38.8	85.2
HHS (excluding SSA in 1992)	3.1	62.5	68.9	3.6	65.2	77.6	3.6	65.8	84.4
Interior	3.5	39.7	68.9	3.5	42.5	80.2	2.9	44.0	89.5
Justice-Treasury-DHS	14.9	49.1	70.5	17.4	47.2	83.7	21.8	41.3	92.3
Transportation	4.1	26.8	69.5	7.3	28.8	78.0	3.3	26.6	86.2
VA	11.2	63.6	80.7	11.8	63.3	86.0	15.7	63.6	86.2

	Dec. 1992			Dec. 2002			Dec. 2012		
	% of Total Pop	% Female	Female/ Male Sal %	% of Total Pop	% Female	Female/ Male Sal %	% of Total Pop	% Female	Female/ Male Sal %
SSA	4.0	70.1	73.2	4.3	70.2	80.5	3.7	67.6	88.9
Other	13.5	45.5	67.9	13.0	46.9	79.5	10.9	47.2	88.1
Population-weighted average			*70.8*			*80.6*			*87.8*
Education									
Below High-School	1.1	63.8	79.2	0.7	67.9	86.9	0.3	66.4	91.8
High School Graduate or Equivalency	22.4	65.5	77.9	24.2	56.9	90.2	22.1	46.9	89.9
Occupational Training/Certificate	5.9	72.0	79.2	4.2	70.7	82.9	3.3	70.2	85.3
Some College (Four Years Or Less)	27.3	55.9	77.6	25.0	55.2	84.3	20.7	51.7	89.3
Bachelor's Degree	24.7	33.9	80.6	26.3	38.2	87.1	29.1	41.9	91.0
Post Bachelor	7.2	27.0	82.8	6.4	33.7	91.0	5.8	41.8	90.4
Master's Degree	8.0	30.2	83.1	9.9	36.3	89.2	14.7	43.8	90.3
Post Master	1.3	23.9	81.6	1.0	29.9	88.7	0.8	41.1	91.1
Doctorate Degree	1.7	18.0	87.5	2.0	25.7	91.9	2.6	38.6	92.4
Post Doctorate	0.3	12.5	87.9	0.3	21.1	89.6	0.4	34.8	91.3
Population-weighted average			*79.6*			*87.5*			*90.1*
Length of Service									
<5	16.9	57.3	77.2	16.2	46.2	87.5	27.0	43.9	88.7
5-9	20.8	53.1	74.1	10.4	44.2	86.5	19.5	43.2	88.1
10-14	17.9	52.3	75.2	16.8	51.0	79.8	14.7	43.1	88.0
15-19	16.1	48.7	74.7	18.5	50.8	77.4	8.0	44.3	86.7
20-24	13.1	40.3	70.6	15.2	51.3	79.1	11.0	51.0	82.0
25-29	9.1	38.3	69.0	12.5	46.7	80.4	10.2	52.0	80.8
30-34	4.2	26.4	69.0	7.5	38.4	78.5	5.9	54.5	82.2
35+	1.8	25.9	67.6	3.1	39.5	75.3	3.6	52.7	81.4
Population-weighted average			*73.7*			*81.0*			*86.1*
Occupational Category #1 (PATCO)									

	Dec. 1992				Dec. 2002				Dec. 2012	
	% of Total Pop	% Female	Female/ Male Sal %	% of Total Pop	% Female	Female/ Male Sal %	% of Total Pop	% Female	Female/ Male Sal %
A-Administrative	32.7	39.8	83.3	40.0	44.8	88.7	43.6	42.8	94.5
C-Clerical	15.8	86.2	108.1	7.5	82.1	111.4	5.3	69.0	110.4
O-Other White Collar	2.7	9.8	84.8	3.6	10.8	90.4	4.4	11.6	85.8
P-Professional	26.5	33.1	80.7	26.2	38.2	85.5	28.0	45.0	88.2
T-Technical	22.3	56.8	78.5	22.8	58.1	86.4	18.7	57.6	87.0
Population-weighted average			*85.5*			*89.1*			*91.8*
Occupational Category #2 (PATCO + Occ Family)									
00xx-A Misc (Admin)	1.5	28.8	88.2	1.8	33.4	96.6	1.8	32.5	101.7
00xx-O Misc (Other)	2.2	6.8	97.3	2.6	9.3	99.8	2.8	9.7	100.2
01xx-A Social Science (Admin)	1.9	57.0	85.1	2.6	61.4	91.5	2.7	58.4	91.4
01xx-P Social Science (Prof)	1.5	35.8	80.4	1.8	43.7	87.1	2.2	57.8	89.4
02xx-A Personnel Mgmt (Admin)	1.9	60.7	83.9	1.9	70.1	89.5	1.8	69.8	100.2
03xx-A General Admin/Clerical (Admin)	7.8	47.3	79.1	9.9	55.3	85.3	12.2	51.7	91.8
03xx-C General Admin/Clerical (Clerical)	10.9	88.6	112.2	5.3	85.0	115.3	2.4	78.9	116.7
03xx-T General Admin/Clerical (Tech)	3.6	74.9	94.1	3.7	79.1	98.8	2.9	74.2	102.1
04xx-P Natural Resources (Prof)	2.3	19.8	83.7	2.5	27.5	90.3	2.2	35.5	96.7
05xx-A Accounting & Budget (Admin)	1.9	55.4	77.3	2.5	63.4	79.9	2.8	62.7	88.7
05xx-P Accounting & Budget (Prof)	2.9	36.2	82.9	2.5	44.4	88.1	2.3	52.7	94.9
05xx-T Accounting & Budget (Tech)	3.3	79.7	99.9	2.1	79.1	102.3	1.6	74.2	103.3
06xx-C Medical/Health (Clerical)	0.7	81.1	101.8	0.6	79.1	100.9	1.1	72.4	101.8
0602-0680-P Doctor/Dentist (Prof)	0.6	20.9	96.5	0.7	27.5	98.2	1.1	35.5	92.7
06xx-P* Medical/Health (Prof-other + 0603A)	3.9	76.8	93.2	4.6	73.4	94.2	6.1	75.2	94.8

	Dec. 1992			Dec. 2002			Dec. 2012		
	% of Total Pop	% Female	Female/Male Sal %	% of Total Pop	% Female	Female/Male Sal %	% of Total Pop	% Female	Female/Male Sal %
06xx-T Medical/Health (Tech)	3.6	67.2	90.6	3.4	70.0	94.8	4.2	71.4	94.6
08xx-P Engineering/Architecture (Prof)	7.3	9.2	84.0	6.4	11.7	91.8	6.1	15.6	94.9
08xx-T Engineering/Architecture (Tech)	3.1	7.7	80.0	2.1	8.6	87.9	1.6	8.3	92.5
09xx-A Legal (Admin)	1.2	58.5	80.5	1.5	65.4	89.4	1.8	62.4	102.3
09xx-P Legal (Prof)	1.6	32.9	87.4	1.9	38.7	92.1	2.1	45.0	94.1
09xx-T Legal (Tech)	1.5	78.4	97.1	2.5	78.4	101.5	2.0	73.3	105.1
11xx-A Business/Industry (Admin)	2.6	39.1	83.0	2.9	45.7	88.4	2.5	48.1	93.9
11xx-P Business/Industry (Prof)	2.0	56.4	84.4	1.9	60.8	90.5	2.2	56.4	100.5
11xx-T Business/Industry (Tech)	1.4	62.5	77.0	1.2	65.0	83.0	0.9	55.7	90.6
13xx-P Physical Sciences (Prof)	2.2	16.9	82.0	1.9	21.1	88.0	1.5	26.9	91.8
15xx-P Mathematics/Statistics (Prof)	0.8	27.8	85.0	0.9	32.3	91.1	1.0	32.5	95.0
18xx-AO Investigation (Admin + 1896&1899 O)	4.1	18.2	84.1	6.3	20.2	96.8	8.0	19.5	99.4
18xx-T Investigation (Tech)	0.8	33.2	79.7	1.1	49.9	91.0	2.2	43.6	99.4
21xx-A Transportation (Admin)	2.1	16.4	83.8	2.7	16.4	89.9	2.1	17.3	95.7
2181-2183-T Pilot/Navigator (Tech)	0.2	1.1	90.5	0.2	1.9	91.1	0.2	1.6	101.7
21xx-T* Transportation (Tech-other)	0.2	42.6	87.0	0.3	50.5	86.3	0.2	40.3	89.2
22xx-A Information Technology (Admin)	3.4	38.6	87.2	4.6	39.7	94.9	4.8	30.7	101.8
Xxxx-P All other Prof	1.3	48.1	78.6	1.3	44.0	85.4	1.4	40.6	92.0
Xxxx-A All other Admin	4.6	32.7	87.5	3.9	37.2	95.5	4.2	34.8	103.9
Xxxx-T All other Tech	4.7	50.0	85.8	6.1	42.8	96.4	2.9	43.9	96.1
Xxxx-C All other Clerical	4.1	80.6	100.6	1.6	73.1	101.1	1.8	53.3	101.9
Xxxx-O All other Other	0.2	48.5	96.0	0.2	48.1	101.1	0.3	55.8	100.3
Population-weighted average			89.5			93.7			97.1
Pay System									
General Schedule (GS, GL, GM)	92.9	48.2	70.3	83.3	49.7	81.6	80.7	47.4	89.2

Appendix 3. (Continued)

	Dec. 1992			Dec. 2002			Dec. 2012		
	% of Total Pop	% Female	Female/ Male Sal %	% of Total Pop	% Female	Female/ Male Sal %	% of Total Pop	% Female	Female/ Male Sal %
Senior Executive Service (ES)	0.5	12.6	97.6	0.5	25.5	99.4	0.5	33.2	99.2
VA nurse [VN]	2.2	86.2	99.8	2.4	82.8	100.0	3.2	81.5	100.7
Other	4.4	36.8	69.1	13.8	30.3	82.0	15.6	33.5	88.3
Population-weighted average			71.0			82.2			89.5
Race/Ethnicity									
American Indian/Alaskan Native	1.6	59.8	71.0	1.8	60.7	74.8	1.6	61.9	79.2
Asian & Native Hawaiian/Pacific Islander	2.8	47.3	77.1	4.0	48.1	83.5	5.8	47.8	90.8
Black/African American	16.3	69.9	81.0	17.3	67.7	89.8	18.0	63.4	95.2
Hispanic/Latino	5.1	48.2	76.4	6.9	45.5	86.9	8.2	43.1	91.0
White	73.6	43.4	69.9	69.3	42.6	80.3	65.3	41.3	87.1
Other	0.6	45.5	69.0	0.6	44.8	78.2	1.0	48.0	90.4
Population-weighted average			72.3			82.4			89.0
Supervisor Status									
Manager/Supervisor	14.9	28.8	77.9	12.4	33.2	89.8	13.7	36.0	95.6
Non-supervisor	85.1	51.7	72.8	87.6	49.7	81.4	86.3	47.9	88.0
Population-weighted average			73.6			82.4			89.1

Note: OPM collected similar data on other factors--bargaining unit status, disability status, duty station, law enforcement officer status, and veteran status--which are not presented in this report for sake of brevity.

APPENDIX 4.

Snapshot Data by General Schedule Grade Level

GS-GL-GM nonseasonal full-time permanent employees in pay status in the Executive Branch

a. Summary for 1992, 2002, and 2012

	Dec. 1992			Dec. 2002			Dec. 2012		
	% of Total Pop	% Female	Female/Male Sal %	% of Total Pop	% Female	Female/Male Sal %	% of Total Pop	% Female	Female/Male Sal %
Total GS Pop.	100.0	48.2	70.3	100.0	49.7	81.6	100.0	47.4	89.2
Grade Level									
1-3 combined	1.3	66.5	98.5	0.4	60.8	99.8	0.2	59.9	99.9
4	6.3	76.3	99.7	2.7	68.4	100.2	1.7	65.7	100.8
5	11.2	77.1	100.9	7.7	67.3	101.6	5.5	63.6	101.8
6	7.2	77.1	101.4	6.5	70.5	101.8	5.6	65.8	102.1
7	10.0	65.6	100.5	10.3	64.7	100.4	5.6	55.8	101.3
8	2.3	59.5	100.0	4.1	64.3	98.6	8.8	59.6	98.7
9	10.4	48.4	97.4	10.1	53.8	98.7	4.0	49.5	101.0
10	2.1	53.1	99.4	1.4	47.9	100.6	9.4	51.5	103.7
11	13.7	39.0	96.1	14.8	46.4	98.4	1.2	48.4	100.9
12	15.9	30.1	95.3	17.4	41.5	97.4	14.3	40.9	101.6
13	10.9	23.9	95.4	14.6	35.7	97.4	20.3	38.9	100.0
14	5.9	18.6	95.8	6.6	32.6	97.4	16.9	38.9	99.5
15	2.7	14.6	95.5	3.4	28.3	97.6	8.1	35.5	99.5
Pop.-weighted avg.			97.8			98.8	4.0		100.8

b. Detailed Data for December 2012

General Schedule (GS-GL-GM)

Nonseasonal Full-Time Permanent Employees in Pay Status in the Executive Branch by GS Grade Level

GS Grade Level	Total Empl	% of Total Pop	# Male Empl	# Female Empl	% Female	Avg Sal	Male Avg Sal	Female Avg Sal	Female/ Male Sal %
1-3 combined	3,095	0.2%	1,241	1,854	59.9%	$29,363	$29,382	$29,351	99.9%
4	23,436	1.7%	8,040	15,396	65.7%	$33,405	$33,239	$33,492	100.8%
5	73,574	5.5%	26,817	46,757	63.6%	$37,412	$36,992	$37,653	101.8%
6	75,337	5.6%	25,733	49,604	65.8%	$42,489	$41,916	$42,787	102.1%
7	118,291	8.8%	52,231	66,060	55.8%	$47,086	$46,755	$47,347	101.3%
8	54,536	4.0%	22,026	32,510	59.6%	$53,443	$53,873	$53,151	98.7%
9	126,172	9.4%	63,669	62,503	49.5%	$56,698	$56,412	$56,989	101.0%
10	15,622	1.2%	7,584	8,038	51.5%	$64,422	$63,227	$65,550	103.7%
11	192,716	14.3%	99,389	93,327	48.4%	$68,072	$67,785	$68,377	100.9%
12	273,368	20.3%	161,655	111,713	40.9%	$82,238	$81,696	$83,021	101.6%
13	228,233	16.9%	139,491	88,742	38.9%	$100,266	$100,282	$100,240	100.0%
14	108,940	8.1%	66,558	42,382	38.9%	$121,017	$121,276	$120,609	99.5%
15	54,042	4.0%	34,877	19,165	35.5%	$145,114	$145,366	$144,656	99.5%
Total	1,347,362	100.0%	709,311	638,051	47.4%	$76,432	$80,569	$71,833	89.2%
Female avg salary as % of male avg salary - based on population-weighted avg of subpopulation avg %'s:									100.8%

APPENDIX 5.

Summary of Dynamic Data Findings

Nonseasonal full-time permanent employees in the Executive Branch.
a. Superior Qualification Actions, Quality Step Increases, and Promotions

General Schedule (GS) or White Collar (WC)

	1992				2002				2012			
	% of actions used for females	% of total population that are female	actions for males as % of male population	actions for females as % of female population	% of actions used for females	% of total population that are female	actions for males as % of male population	actions for females as % of female population	% of actions used for females	% of total population that are female	actions for males as % of male population	actions for females as % of female population
Superior Qualification Actions - GS*	36.4	49.1	2.7	1.6	31.3	43.6	9.1	5.4	34.9	44.8	12.6	8.3
Quality Step Increases - GS	58.0	48.3	3.10	4.58	51.8	49.8	4.78	5.18	50.7	47.5	3.11	3.53
Promotions (excluding temporary & others) - WC	58.7	48.4	4.69	7.10	51.8	48.0	5.66	6.58	50.1	46.3	3.38	3.94
Promotions (excluding temporary & others) - GS	58.8	48.3	5.00	7.63	52.4	49.8	6.48	7.21	50.4	47.5	4.05	4.55

* For superior qualification actions, the "population" eligible for possible use of the action is the population of new hires.

b. Starting Salaries

	1992			2002			2012		
	% of total new hires by subpop.	% of new hires that are female	% female / male avg salary	% of total new hires by subpop.	% of new hires that are female	% female / male avg salary	% of total new hires by subpop.	% of new hires that are female	% female / male avg salary
Total Population - White Collar	100.0	49.3	83.1	100.0	38.0	89.4	100.0	45.0	89.3
Occupational Category #1 (PATCO)									
A-Administrative	19.6	35.0	91.9	22.7	27.6	92.6	30.9	30.0	97.2
C-Clerical	23.0	77.4	107.0	7.4	74.9	105.3	9.2	60.0	102.7
O-Other White Collar	13.2	28.9	87.4	8.5	20.7	93.0	8.5	27.3	96.3
P-Professional	25.7	44.4	88.8	17.4	40.8	90.6	30.3	52.7	88.6
T-Technical	18.5	50.8	87.3	44.1	39.4	94.8	21.1	56.6	86.9
Weighted average:			93.1			94.2			92.9
Total Population - General Schedule	100.0	49.1	83.8	100.0	43.6	87.4	100.0	44.8	90.0
Occupational Category #1 (PATCO)									
A-Administrative	18.4	34.4	93.2	27.8	33.5	93.5	30.6	30.3	96.9
C-Clerical	24.4	77.3	106.8	12.5	74.3	104.4	10.5	60.6	102.1
O-Other White Collar	14.0	29.1	87.6	14.6	20.7	92.8	9.7	26.7	95.8
P-Professional	23.8	41.9	91.2	24.1	41.4	92.5	24.5	51.1	97.0
T-Technical	19.4	50.9	88.8	21.0	57.3	87.4	24.7	57.0	87.8
Weighted average:			94.4			93.2			95.1

End Notes

[1] See Presidential Memorandum--Advancing Pay Equality in the Federal Government and Learning from Successful Practices, May 10, 2013, at http://www.whitehouse.gov/the-press-office/2013/05/10/presidential-memorandumadvancing-pay-equality-federal-government-and-le.

[2] See OPM Memorandum--Request for Information on Pay and Promotion Policies and Practices Relating to Gender Pay Equality, May 10, 2013, at http://www. chcoc.gov/ transmittals/ TransmittalDetails.aspx?TransmittalID=5478.

[3] The term "equivalent-level employees" refers to white-collar employees who are not in executive or senior-level positions. This term excludes employees in blue collar prevailing rate pay systems (i.e., craft, trades, and laboring prevailing rate pay systems with pay set under 5 U.S.C. 5341 et. seq., such as the Federal Wage System or crews of vessels under section 5348); Executive Schedule, Senior Executive Service, and senior-level and scientific and professional positions; administrative law judges; administrative appeals judges; members of boards of contract appeals; and employees in any equivalent pay systems. Experts, consultants, and advisory committee members were also excluded from agency reviews.

[4] See http://www.fedscope.opm.gov/datadefn/aehri sdm.asp for additional information on EHRI-SDM.

[5] For purposes of our data analysis, the "General Schedule" population included the core General Schedule pay plans GS (standard), GL (law enforcement officers at grades 3-10), and GM (for those who were formerly covered by a special managerial pay system), but excluded pay plans GP and GR, which cover doctors and dentists receiving title 38 market pay.

[6] Our regression-decomposition analysis was similar to the analysis that the Government Accountability Office (GAO) performed for its report "Women's Pay: Gender Pay Gap in the Federal Workforce Narrows as Differences in Occupation, Education, and Experience Diminish" (March 2009) at http://www.gao.gov/products/GAO-09-279. GAO performed analyses using September data for 1988, 1998, and 2007. There were some differences between the GAO and OPM analyses in terms of the populations studied and the factors used. For example, the OPM analysis excluded blue-collar employees and used more discrete occupational categories.

[7] Educational level may not be updated after the time of hiring; thus, education level may be understated for some employees. However, OPM and GAO have concluded that the assignment of general education groups (instead of using all possible codes)—such as done in our data analysis—is sufficiently reliable to justify inclusion of this data element in this kind of statistical study.

[8] The PATCO codes provide a very broad description of the type of occupation: Professional (P), Administrative (A), Technical (T), Clerical (C), and Other White Collar (O).

[9] An "occupational family" or "job family" is a set of occupational series in the same numbered range. White-collar occupational series range from 0001-2299. Each range of hundreds (e.g., 02xx or 0201-0299) is an occupational family.

[10] In making pay or salary comparisons, we are using adjusted basic pay, which is base pay plus any applicable locality payment or special rate supplement. In comparing female to male salaries, we used male salaries as the base for comparison. Thus, in this report, we express the average female salary as a percentage of the average male salary. For example, for the overall White Collar population (all pay plans) in December 2012, the average female salary was 87.3 percent of the average male salary. The shorthand term used in this report

for this percentage is the "female salary percentage." In addition, the gender pay disparity or "pay gap" is expressed in this report as a percentage by (1) subtracting the average male salary from the average female salary and (2) dividing the resulting difference by the average male salary. If the female salary percentage is already computed, 100 percent is subtracted from the female salary percentage to derive the pay gap percentage. For example, if the female salary percentage is 87.3 percent, the pay gap is -12.7 percent (87.3 - 100 = -12.7). In other words, the average female salary is 12.7 percent below the average male salary. (In this report, we show the overall pay gap as a positive number, since it is understood that the gap represents the degree to which female pay is below male pay.)

[11] Due to the small populations for grades 1, 2, and 3, those grades were merged to form a single subpopulation; resulting in 13 grade levels instead of 15.

[12] The regression-decomposition analysis produced estimated pay gaps. Because the regression-decomposition method required logarithmic conversions, these estimated gaps do not exactly match the actual overall gaps.

[13] See pages 3, 24, 37, 43, 44, 45, 53, and 98 in the March 2009 report "Women's Pay: Gender Pay Gap in the Federal Workforce Narrows as Differences in Occupation, Education, and Experience Diminish" (GAO-09-279).

[14] See salaries and wages at http://www.opm.gov/policy-data-oversight/pay-leave/salaries-wages/.

[15] See superior qualifications and special needs pay-setting authority fact sheet at http://www.opm.gov/policy-dataoversight/pay-leave/pay-administration/fact-sheets/superior-qualifications-and-special-needs-pay-setting-authority/ and maximum payable rate fact sheet at http://www.opm.gov/policy-data-oversight/pay-leave/payadministration/fact-sheets/maximum-payable-rate-rule/.

[16] See GS classification and pay fact sheet at http://www.opm.gov/policy-data-oversight/pay-leave/paysystems/general-schedule/.

[17] HR University is accessible at www.hru.gov.

[18] Current videos are available at http://www.youtube.com/user/usajobsapp.

[19] June 2013 FedScope data. FedScope is available at http://www.opm.gov/policy-data-oversight/data-analysisdocumentation/fedscope/.

In: The Equal Pay Act, Fifty Years on   ISBN: 978-1-63463-730-5
Editor: Suzanna Cross   © 2015 Nova Science Publishers, Inc.

Chapter 3

WHY DO WOMEN STILL EARN LESS THAN MEN?*

Lawrence H. Leith

The earnings gap that exists between men and women is a widely discussed and debated topic. The Bureau of Labor Statistics recently reported that median weekly earnings for women who usually worked full time in 2012 were 82.8 percent of what their male counterparts earned. Although women have narrowed the gap considerably over the last several decades—in 1979, women's weekly earnings were just 62.3 percent of men's—the question of why women continue to earn less than men remains a concern among policymakers, employers, and the general population. In "A grand gender convergence: its last chapter" (American Economic Review, April 2014), economist Claudia Goldin, who has conducted extensive research on women's labor market issues and published numerous scholarly articles on the topic, assesses the existing research on the "earnings gap" and provides data from her own work to support her argument for how the gap might be eliminated entirely in the future.

Since at least the beginning of the twentieth century, there has been what Goldin calls a "grand convergence" in gender roles in society, with women making major strides toward political and economic equality. Several decades of research have shed much light on the issue of labor market disparities

---

* This is an edited, reformatted and augmented version of a Monthly Labor Review article, issued by the U.S. Bureau of Labor Statistics, June 2014.

between women and men, with many studies showing that the earnings gap is narrower in some occupations or when the researchers "control" for certain variables that tend to drive earnings, such as education, work experience, and total time spent in the labor force. In other words, among women and men with similar "human capital" characteristics, the earnings gap narrows substantially and in some cases nearly disappears.

Nevertheless, earnings differences between women and men persist, and researchers have suggested a number of explanations for the disparity. As Goldin notes, the research on this issue has produced an "explained" portion of the gender earnings gap and a "residual" portion, the latter often called "wage discrimination"—women earn less simply because they are women. The part of the gap that can be explained relates primarily to human capital investments. In the past, men tended to have more education, training, and work experience than women, which partly explains why they earned more. But women have made substantial advances in each of these areas. About half of all current law and medical students, for example, are women, and among students enrolled in programs in the biological sciences, pharmacy, and veterinary medicine, women actually outnumber men. As women have increased their human capital and enhanced their labor market potential, their earnings have risen relative to those of men, thus narrowing the gap. In certain occupations, women with comparable levels of education and work experience earn nearly as much as men. In general, however, women's earnings continue to lag those of men—that is, even after adjusting for differences in education and work experience, the earnings gap remains.

In her summary of the existing research on the gender earnings gap, Goldin argues that while many of the studies' explanations have considerable merit, a residual (unexplained) portion of the gap remains. A number of studies have shown, for example, that women tend to have less ability in bargaining and are not as competitive as men; hence, they accept lower earnings than their male counterparts. Other studies have argued that employers have different hiring and promotion standards for women because they are more likely than men to leave the job (or to leave sooner than men, on average). But these studies do not explain why women with no children earn more than those with children, other things equal. They also do not explain why the economic penalties for time out of the labor force or for working fewer hours per day or week than men vary radically for different occupations.

As Goldin argues, there are wide disparities within some occupations while others have achieved relative equity, and this is the key to eliminating the gender earnings gap. In some occupations, such as that of pharmacist, the earnings gap is small and the penalty for working fewer hours or taking time out of the labor force is low. In other occupations, particularly those categorized as "business" occupations, the gap is large and the penalty is high. In general, science, technology, and health occupations have relatively more flexibility in the workplace than business and other occupations, especially concerning the number of hours worked each day or week, the particular hours worked, and the economic penalties workers pay for taking time off from work.

As the author points out, the earnings gap is much smaller for young women and men at the beginning of their careers, especially among college graduates with comparable levels of training and experience. Then, as people age and enter into marital and family relationships—and women become more likely to temporarily leave the labor force—the gap widens sharply. It finally begins to narrow again as workers age and move beyond the childbearing years. Since women disproportionately pay a penalty for working fewer hours or for taking time off from work, the solution to the earnings gap is for all occupations and industries to adopt workplace practices that are more flexible around these issues.

What needs to happen, according to Goldin, is for the entire economy to move in the direction of greater "temporal flexibility" in the workplace, especially with regard to how workers' time is allocated and how they are compensated; the achievement of this will "require changes in the structure of work" so that the costs associated with increased flexibility are reduced. This has already occurred in many occupations and sectors. Among pharmacists, for example, women and men earn nearly equal pay on a per-hour basis, after adjusting for differences in human capital characteristics. Many firms in health care, retail sales, banking, and real estate have also shifted toward greater flexibility, with women and men becoming better substitutes for one another, despite their different temporal demands. In addition, self-employment has declined in many of the traditional professions, which has led to a reduction in the premium paid for working unpredictably long hours in those occupations. Although there will always be certain jobs for which temporal flexibility is not an option, if employers had less incentive to reward people for working long hours or being "on call" and more incentive for allowing their employees greater flexibility, the earnings gap between women and men could be eliminated, at least in most sectors of the economy.

In: The Equal Pay Act, Fifty Years on   ISBN: 978-1-63463-730-5
Editor: Suzanna Cross   © 2015 Nova Science Publishers, Inc.

Chapter 4

PAY EQUITY: LEGISLATIVE AND LEGAL DEVELOPMENTS*

Benjamin Collins and Jody Feder

SUMMARY

The term "pay gap" refers to the difference in earnings between male and female workers. While the pay gap has narrowed since the 1960s, female workers with a strong attachment to the labor force earn about 77 to 81 cents for every dollar earned by similar male workers. Studies have analyzed the earnings and characteristics of male and female workers and found that a substantial portion of the pay gap is attributable to non-gender factors such as occupation and employment tenure. Some interpret these studies as evidence that discrimination, if present at all, is a minor factor in the pay gap and conclude that no policy changes are necessary. Conversely, advocates for further policy interventions note that some of the explanatory factors of the pay gap (such as occupation and hours worked) could be the result of discrimination and that no broadly accepted methodology is able to attribute the entirety of the pay gap to non-gender factors.

The Equal Pay Act (EPA), which amends the Fair Labor Standards Act (FLSA), prohibits covered employers from paying lower wages to female employees than male employees for "equal work" on jobs

---

* This is an edited, reformatted and augmented version of a Congressional Research Service publication RL31867, prepared for Members and Committees of Congress, dated November 22, 2013.

requiring "equal skill, effort, and responsibility" and performed "under similar working conditions" at the same location. The FLSA exempts some jobs (e.g., hotel service workers) from EPA coverage, and the EPA makes exceptions for wage differentials based on merit or seniority systems, systems that measure earnings by "quality or quantity" of production, or "any factor other than sex." The "equal work" standard embodies a middle ground between demanding that two jobs either be exactly alike or that they merely be comparable. The test applied by the courts focuses on job similarity and whether, given all the circumstances, they require substantially the same skill, effort, and responsibility. The EPA may be enforced by the government, or individual complainants, in civil actions for wages unlawfully withheld and liquidated damages for willful violations. In addition, Title VII of the 1964 Civil Rights Act provides for the awarding of compensatory and punitive damages to victims of "intentional" wage discrimination, subject to caps on the employer's monetary liability.

The issue of pay equity has attracted substantial attention in recent Congresses. A number of measures, including bills that would provide additional remedies, mandate "equal pay for equivalent jobs," or require studies on pay inequity, have been introduced in each of the last several congressional sessions. These bills include the Paycheck Fairness Act (H.R. 377/S. 84) and the Fair Pay Act (H.R. 438/S. 168) in the 113th Congress. This report also discusses pay equity litigation, including *Wal-Mart Stores v. Dukes*, a case in which the Supreme Court rejected class action status for current and former female Wal-Mart employees who allege that the company has engaged in pay discrimination.

The persistence of gender-based wage disparities—commonly referred to as the pay or wage gap—has been the subject of extensive debate and commentary. Congress first addressed the issue more than four decades ago in the Equal Pay Act of 1963,[1] mandating an "equal pay for equal work" standard, and addressed it again the following year in Title VII of the 1964 Civil Rights Act.[2] Collection of compensation data and elimination of male/female pay disparities are also integral to Labor Department enforcement of Executive Order 11246 (initially issued by President Lyndon Johnson), which mandates nondiscrimination and affirmative action by federal contractors. During the last several decades, initiatives to strengthen and expand current federal remedies available to victims of unlawful sex-based wage discrimination have been taken up in Congress.

This report begins by presenting data trends in earnings for male and female workers and by discussing explanations that have been offered for the differences in earnings. It next discusses the major laws directed at eliminating sex-based wage discrimination as well as relevant federal court cases. The report closes with a description of pay equity legislation that has been considered or enacted by Congress in recent years.

EARNINGS TRENDS AMONG MALE AND FEMALE WORKERS

Historical and Recent Data

This section uses two commonly cited federal data sources to discuss the earnings of full-time male and female workers.[3] The Census Bureau publishes data on the median annual earnings of full-time, year-round workers (i.e., at least 35 hours per week and at least 50 weeks per year). These data include workers age 15 and over and are available beginning in 1960. The Bureau of Labor Statistics (BLS) publishes data on the median weekly earnings of full-time workers (i.e., at least 35 hours per week, including part-year workers). These data include workers age 16 and over and are available beginning in 1979.

Figure 1 uses these two data series to chart median female earnings as a percentage of median male earnings. The weekly wage gap has tended to be slightly smaller than the annual wage gap, though both have trended similarly. Considerations related to interpreting these data are discussed in the next section of this report.

In 2012, the median annual earnings for female workers who worked full-time, year round were 76.5% of male workers with a similar level of labor force attachment ($49,398 v. $37,791).[4] Using the weekly wage metric, female workers' median earnings in 2012 were 80.9% of male workers' ($691 v. $854).[5]

Another BLS publication estimated the median weekly earnings in 2011 for full-time male and female workers in various demographic groups. Some demographic groups had smaller wage gaps than the overall working population while others had larger gaps. For example, among workers between the ages of 25 and 34, female workers' earnings were 92.3% of male workers'. Conversely, the earnings of all female workers with at least a bachelor's degree were 74.9% of similarly educated male workers.[6]

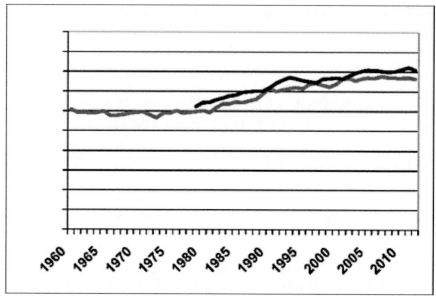

Source: Graph constructed by CRS using data from Income, Poverty, and Health
    Insurance Coverage in the United States: 2012, United States Census Bureau,
    September 2013, Table A-4, http://www.census.gov/prod/2013pubs/p60-245.pdf
    and Employment and Earnings, United States Department of Labor, Bureau of
    Labor Statistics, Table 37, http://www.bls.gov/opub/ee/2013/cps/annavg37
    _2012.pdf.
Notes: Annual earnings data include workers age 15 and over. Weekly earnings data
    include workers age 16 and over. Weekly wage data are not available prior to
    1979.

Figure 1. Female Earnings as a Percentage of Male Earnings, 1960-2012. Full-time
workers, median annual earnings (red line) and median weekly earnings (black line).

Considerations Related to Interpreting Gender Wage Data

Some have attributed the wage differentials discussed in the prior section
to discrimination towards female workers. A significant body of research,
however, has found that a substantial portion of the wage gap can be attributed
to non-gender differences between male and female workers such as
consecutive years in the labor force or the concentration of workers of a single
gender in certain high- or low-paying occupations. While this body of research
suggests that the unexplained portion of the wage gap is smaller than the raw
wage gap discussed in the prior section, there is no broadly accepted

methodology that is able to attribute the entirety of the raw wage gap to factors other than gender.[7]

Typically, studies that examine the wage gap compare the earnings of male and female workers while controlling for observable characteristics that may be related to earnings such as education and occupation. Most studies also consider hourly wages rather than weekly or annual wages to control for variations in the number of hours worked. For example, a frequently cited study by Blau and Kahn used data from 1998 to examine hourly wage differences between male and female workers while controlling for education, experience, occupation, industry, collective bargaining coverage, and other characteristics. When their full model was applied, it estimated an unexplained difference of about 9% between the earnings of male and female workers.[8] Another study, commissioned by the U.S. Department of Labor and using data from 2007, used a different data source from Blau and Kahn and controlled for a slightly different set of personal and human capital characteristics. It found an unexplained earnings differential of between 5% and 7%.[9]

Interpretations of these studies vary. Some view the attribution of substantial portions of the raw pay gap to non-gender factors as evidence that, if present at all, discrimination is a minor factor in the gender wage gap. Others note that many of the explanatory factors (such as occupation and job tenure) could themselves be influenced by discrimination and advocate for further policy interventions.

LEGAL AND LEGISLATIVE BACKGROUND

Laws That Combat Sex-Based Wage Discrimination

The Equal Pay Act (EPA) is a 1963 amendment to the Fair Labor Standards Act that makes it illegal to pay different wages to employees of the opposite sex for equal work on jobs the performance of which requires "equal skill, effort, and responsibility," and which are "performed under similar working conditions."[10] The act also prohibits labor organizations and their agents from causing or attempting to cause sex-based wage discrimination by employers. Specifically permitted by the EPA, however, are wage differentials based on seniority systems, merit systems, systems that measure earnings by quality or quantity of production, or "any factor other than sex."[11] The "equal work" standard embodies a middle ground between demanding that two jobs be either exactly alike or that they merely be comparable. The test applied by the courts focuses on job similarity and whether, in light of all the circumstances, they require substantially the same skill, effort, and responsibility.[12] An employer may not attempt to equalize wages to comply with the EPA by lowering the rate of pay for any employee.[13]

A year after passage of the EPA, Congress enacted the comprehensive code of anti-discrimination rules based on race, color, national origin, religion, and sex found in Title VII of the Civil Rights Act. The EPA and Title VII provide overlapping coverage for claims of sex-based wage discrimination, but differ in important substantive, procedural, and remedial aspects. A crucial difference is that the "equal work" standard of the EPA—requiring "substantial" identity between compared male and female jobs—does not limit an employer's liability for intentional wage discrimination under Title VII. For example, in *Miranda v. B & B Cash Grocery Store, Inc.,*[14] the plaintiff's inability to demonstrate that she performed the same work as higher paid males did not preclude a Title VII claim based on evidence male employees who performed fewer duties were paid more than she, or that the employer would have paid her more had she been a male. Thus, a violation of the EPA will generally violate Title VII, but the converse is not true.[15]

Additionally, the remedies for violation of the two laws differ. Under the EPA, a prevailing plaintiff may obtain backpay for any wages unlawfully withheld as the result of pay inequality and twice that amount in liquidated damages for a willful violation. By contrast, the Civil Rights Act of 1991 added to the backpay remedy authorized by Title VII a provision for jury trials and compensatory and punitive damages for victims of "intentional" sex discrimination in wage cases and otherwise.[16] Such damages may only be recovered, however, in cases of intentional discrimination, not in so-called "disparate impact" cases alleging the adverse effect of a facially neutral employment practice on a protected group member. In addition, the Title VII damages remedy is limited by dollar "caps," which vary depending on the size of the employer.[17]

The *Ledbetter* Case and Subsequent Legislation

In 2007, the Supreme Court issued a decision in *Ledbetter v. Goodyear Tire & Rubber Co., Inc.,*[18] a case in which the female plaintiff alleged that past sex discrimination had resulted in lower pay increases and that these past pay decisions continued to affect the amount of her pay throughout her employment, resulting in a significant pay disparity between her and her male colleagues by the end of her nearly 20-year career. Under Title VII, plaintiffs are required to file suit within 180 days "after the alleged unlawful employment practice occurred."[19] Although the plaintiff argued that each paycheck she received constituted a new violation of the statute and therefore reset the clock with regard to filing a claim, the Court rejected this argument, reasoning that "a new violation does not occur, and a new charging period does not commence, upon the occurrence of subsequent nondiscriminatory acts that entail adverse effects resulting from the past discrimination."[20] As a result, the Court held that the plaintiff had not filed suit in a timely manner. Initially, the decision appeared to limit some pay discrimination claims based on Title VII, but did not affect an individual's ability to sue for sex discrimination that results in pay bias under the Equal Pay Act, which does not contain the 180-day filing deadline.

Although the Court's decision made it more difficult for employees to sue for pay discrimination under Title VII, the ruling was subsequently superseded by the Lilly Ledbetter Fair Pay Act of 2009, which amended Title VII to clarify that the time limit for suing employers for pay discrimination begins each time they issue a paycheck and is not limited to the original discriminatory action.[21] This change is applicable not only to Title VII of the Civil Rights Act, but also to the Age Discrimination in Employment Act (ADEA), the Rehabilitation Act of 1973, and the Americans with Disabilities Act (ADA).[22]

The Wal-Mart Case

In 2004, a federal district court permitted to proceed a class action on behalf of more than 1.5 million current and former female employees of Wal-Mart retail stores nationwide. In *Dukes et al.v. Wal-Mart Stores, Inc.*,[23] the plaintiffs claim that women over the past five years have been paid less than male workers in comparable positions and that the company systematically passed over female employees when awarding promotions to management. According to two studies conducted by a sociologist and a statistician for the plaintiffs, 65% of Wal-Mart's hourly employees were women, but women made up only 33% of all management positions. The gender gap was even more striking when employment categories were further broken down; while the vast majority of Wal-Mart's cashiers were women, only a small fraction were store managers, the top in-store management position. The studies also found that women employed on a full-time hourly basis earned less per year on average than their male counterparts, and the shortfall was substantial for female store managers.

At this initial stage, the district court considered only whether the evidence raised issues of law and fact common to all members of the proposed class sufficient for a class action to proceed under federal law. The court did not decide the merits of plaintiffs' discrimination claims or any issue of Wal-Mart liability. In its opinion, however, the court noted:

> Plaintiffs present largely uncontested descriptive statistics which show that women working at Wal-Mart stores are paid less than men in every region, that pay disparities exist in most job categories, that the salary gap widens over time, that women take longer to enter management positions, and that the higher one looks in the organization the lower the percentage of women.[24]

Wal-Mart argued that any disparities were the result of decentralized decision-making at the regional and local level, not the result of any systematic employer bias, and that a massive class-action would be too large to administer. The court rejected that argument, however, noting that Title VII "contains no special exception for large employers." Moreover, "[i]nsulating our nation's largest employers from allegations that they have engaged in a pattern or practice of gender or racial discrimination—simply because they are large—would seriously undermine these imperatives."[25] Thus, any "inference" of discrimination in company compensation and promotion policies was found to "affect all plaintiffs in a common manner," and warranted the requested class certification.[26]

Wal-Mart appealed the district court's class action certification, and a three-judge panel of the appellate court upheld the class action certification,[27] as did a subsequent ruling by a divided panel of appellate judges sitting en banc.[28] In a 5-4 decision in *Wal-Mart v. Dukes*, however, the Supreme Court recently reversed the class certification ruling.[29]

Under the Federal Rules of Civil Procedure, parties seeking class certification must show, among other things, that

> (1) the class is so numerous that joinder of all members is impracticable, (2) there are questions of law or fact common to the class, (3) the claims or defenses of the representative parties are typical of the claims or defenses of the class, and (4) the representative parties will fairly and adequately protect the interests of the class.[30]

According to the Court, the *Dukes* plaintiffs failed to meet the commonality requirement because they could not establish that Wal-Mart operated under a common, general policy of discrimination. Rather:

> The only corporate policy that the plaintiffs' evidence convincingly establishes is WalMart's "policy" of allowing discretion by local supervisors over employment matters. On its face, of course, that is just the opposite of a uniform employment practice that would provide the commonality needed for a class action.[31]

In its ruling, the Court emphasized that plaintiffs must provide "significant proof" that a "specific employment practice" led to the discrimination, and rejected as insufficient statistical and anecdotal evidence offered by the plaintiffs.[32] Although the Court's decision makes it more difficult for employees to receive class certification and thus makes it less likely that large employers will face similar suits in the future, it is not necessarily the end of the litigation. Plaintiffs may still pursue their claims as individuals, or perhaps as part of a smaller class.

Indeed, approximately 2,000 claimants filed individual charges with the Equal Employment Opportunity Commission (EEOC) within a year of the *Dukes* decision,[33] while others have filed new class action lawsuits that limit claims to stores located in a specified region, such as a single state. These states include California, Texas, Tennessee, and Florida.[34] These lawsuits, however, have not met with much success. In the California case, for example, the district court recently denied the plaintiffs' request for certification of a class consisting of 150,000 women working in Wal-Mart's California stores. According to the court, the "newly proposed class continues to suffer from the problems that foreclosed certification of the nationwide class."[35] Meanwhile, the plaintiffs who refiled complaints against Wal-Mart in Texas, Tennessee, and Florida have had their requests for class certification dismissed as time-barred under the statute of limitations,[36] although some of these decisions have been appealed. Because the statute of limitations is tolled for individual claims, these rulings do not preclude the original *Dukes* plaintiffs from filing individual claims, nor do they prevent new plaintiffs with fresh claims from filing class action lawsuits against the company in the future.

Ultimately, if any of the claims against Wal-Mart go to trial, the female plaintiffs carry the burden of proving that the company engaged in an intentional pattern and practice of discriminating in pay and promotions. The record to date suggests that this may be no easy task, in part due to subjectivity in the company's personnel procedures and the fact that, prior to January 2003, the company apparently failed to post or document most available promotion opportunities.[37] There may be limited data on how many employees, male or female, applied for most of these positions. But if they prevail, whether at trial or by settlement, substantial monetary damages may be available to members of the plaintiff class under Title VII.

Prior to the Court's decision in *Dukes*, other large corporations that had been sued for pay discrimination had a tendency to enter into settlement agreements. For example, the investment firm Morgan Stanley reportedly agreed to pay $54 million to settle government claims that it systematically underpaid and failed to promote its women executives. Allegations of sexual harassment were also involved in the case. Beyond $12 million set aside to pay the lead plaintiff, a consent decree provides $40 million for any of about 340 other potential discrimination victims who are able to prove their claims, and another $2 million to establish internal anti-discrimination programs. For a period of three years, the decree required appointment of a firm ombudsman for sex discrimination issues and of an external monitor to review Morgan Stanley's adherence to the settlement and its progress at preventing discrimination.[38] Shortly after settlement in the Morgan Stanley case, both Boeing and Citigroup agreed to settle similar pay equity lawsuits, and Costco was sued for similar reasons.[39]

In contrast to the above corporations, Costco has chosen to defend itself in court. Although a federal district court granted class-action status to the plaintiffs in *Ellis v. Costco Wholesale Corp.*,[40] a federal appeals court subsequently vacated the district court's ruling regarding commonality and, specifically noting the Supreme Court's decision in *Wal-Mart v. Dukes*, remanded the case for reconsideration and application of the proper legal standard for evaluating commonality.[41] Despite the more stringent post-*Dukes* standards for class action certification, the district court ruled in favor of the Costco plaintiffs on remand.[42] In its decision, the court distinguished the facts in the case from those in the *Dukes* lawsuit, noting that the discrimination claims were limited to a much smaller number of plaintiffs seeking specific management positions, that the promotion process was controlled by central management, and that the plaintiffs had identified this process as the specific employment practice that was subject to challenge. According to the court, "[i]t is this 'common direction' and the identification of specific practices ..., in addition to the smaller size and scope of the class, that separates this case from *Dukes*."[43] Thus, the court held that the Costco plaintiffs had demonstrated sufficient commonality to warrant class action status.

RECENT LEGISLATION

Although the Ledbetter legislation discussed above is the only new pay discrimination law enacted by Congress in recent years, the issue of pay equity continues to garner congressional attention. Indeed, a number of measures have been introduced repeatedly in each of the last several congressional sessions. The two most prominent of these are the Paycheck Fairness Act and the Fair Pay Act, both of which are described below.

Paycheck Fairness Act

Introduced in each of the last several congressional sessions, the Paycheck Fairness Act (H.R. 377/S. 84 in the 113th Congress) would increase penalties for employers who pay different wages to men and women for "equal work," and would add programs for training, research, technical assistance, and pay equity employer recognition awards. The legislation would also make it more difficult for employers to avoid EPA liability, and proposed safeguards would protect employees from retaliation for making inquiries or disclosures concerning employee wages and for filing a charge or participating in any manner in EPA proceedings. In short, while this legislation would adhere to current equal work standards of the EPA, it would reform the procedures and remedies for enforcing the law.

Under the EPA, as noted, prevailing plaintiffs may recover backpay in an amount equal to the total difference between wages actually received and those to which they are lawfully entitled and an additional amount equal to the backpay award as liquidated damages.[44] Compensatory damages are not authorized, and consequently, awards do not include sums for physical or mental distress, medical expenses, or other costs.[45] The Paycheck Fairness Act would authorize EPA class actions and "such compensatory and punitive damages as may be appropriate." In addition, the legislation would establish more restrictive standards for proof by employers of an affirmative defense to EPA liability based on any "bona fide factor other than sex." Thus, for a pay factor to be "bona fide," the employer would have to establish that it was "job related," consistent with "business necessity," and not derived from a sex-based differential in compensation, and that the employer's purpose could not be accomplished by less discriminatory alternative means.

Another aspect of EPA enforcement addressed by proposed pay equity bills concerns employer recordkeeping and the conduct of technical assistance, research, and educational programs by federal agencies. For example, the Paycheck Fairness Act would mandate record-keeping and data collection for better enforcement of the law. The measure would direct the EEOC to survey data currently available to the government and, in consultation with sister agencies, to identify additional sources of pay information that may be marshaled to support federal antidiscrimination efforts. The EEOC would be required to issue regulations for the collection of pay data from employers based on sex, race, and ethnicity, taking into consideration the burden placed on employers and the need to protect the confidentiality of required reports. In addition, the Secretary of Labor would be directed to develop job evaluation guidelines based on objective factors of education, skill, independence, and decision-making responsibility for *voluntary* use by employers in eliminating unfair pay disparities between traditionally male- and female-dominated occupations. Technical assistance and a recognition program would be awarded to employers who voluntarily adjust their wage scales pursuant to such a job evaluation. Finally, a "National Award for Pay Equity in the Workplace" would be established to recognize employers who demonstrate "substantial effort to eliminate pay disparities between men and women."

Fair Pay Act

The Fair Pay Act (H.R. 438/S. 168 in the 113th Congress), which has predecessors dating back to the 103rd Congress, would go further than the Paycheck Fairness Act by proposing a fundamental expansion to the scope of the EPA, which is presently confined to sex-based wage differentials, by adding racial and ethnic minorities as protected classes under that law. Intentional wage discrimination against these groups is already prohibited by Title VII. But Title VII and the EPA have different standards of proof, and because proof of intent to discriminate is not required by the "equal pay for equal work" standard of the EPA,[46] it may provide greater protection to minority groups than Title VII in many cases. The EPA's catchall exception, affording employers broad immunity for pay differentials attributable to "factors other than sex," would be significantly narrowed by the Fair Pay Act. A compensatory and punitive damages remedy, without statutory limit, would replace the present EPA backpay and liquidated damages scheme, based on the Fair Labor Standards Act.

Significantly, the Fair Pay Act would also redefine the basic statutory standard of the EPA by requiring employers to pay equal wages regardless of sex, race, or national origin to workers in "equivalent jobs." Unlike the current law, Equal Pay Act claims based on wage disparities between dissimilar jobs—for example, a janitor and a clerk—would be permitted if they are determined to be "equivalent" in some largely undefined manner. By substituting job equivalency for the "equal work standard" in the EPA, the Fair Pay Act arguably could revive legal issues similar to those confronted by the federal courts during the 1980s in so-called "comparable worth" Title VII cases.[47]

Finally, the Fair Pay Act would require all covered employers to maintain comprehensive records of "the method, system, calculations, and other bases used" to set employee wages and to file annual reports with the EEOC detailing the racial, ethnic, and gender composition of the employer's workforce broken down by job classification and wage or salary level. Such reports would be available for "reasonable" inspection and examination upon request of any person, pursuant to EEOC regulations, and could be used by the Commission for such "statistical and research purposes ... as it may deem appropriate." The EEOC would also be required to "carry on a continuing program of research, education, and technical assistance" to implement the proposed ban on racial, ethnic, or gender discrimination between employees working "in equivalent jobs."

End Notes

[1] 29 U.S.C. § 206(d).

[2] 42 U.S.C. §§ 2000e et seq.

[3] Comparisons between the earnings of male and female workers are typically limited to full-time workers. Since female workers are more likely to work part-time, comparisons that include all workers typically produce a pay gap to which a substantial portion is attributable to fewer female workers working full-time.

[4] United States Census Bureau, Income, Poverty, and Health Insurance Coverage in the United States: 2012, September 2013, Table A-4, http://www.census.gov/prod/2013pubs/p60-245.pdf.

[5] Employment and Earnings, United States Department of Labor, Bureau of Labor Statistics, Table 37, http://www.bls.gov/opub/ee/2013/cps/annavg37_2012.pdf.

[6] United States Department of Labor, Bureau of Labor Statistics, Highlights of Women's Earnings in 2011, October 2012, Table 13, http://www.bls.gov/cps/cpswom2011.pdf.

[7] For a summary of some relevant studies, see Natalia Kolesnikova and Yang Liu, "Gender Wage Gap May Be Much Smaller Than Most Think," The Regional Economist, published by the St. Louis Federal Reserve, October 2011, pp. 14-15, http://www.stlouisfed.org/publications/pub_assets/pdf/re/2011/d/gender_wage_gap.pdf.

[8] See Table 2a in Francine D. Blau and Lawrence M. Kahn, "The U.S. Gender Pay Gap in the 1990s: Slowing Convergence," Industrial and Labor Relations Review, vol. 60, no. 1 (October 2006), pp. 45-66.

[9] CONSAD Research Corporation, prepared for the U.S. Department of Labor, An Analysis of the Reasons for the Disparity in Wages Between Men and Women, January 2009, http://www.consad.com/content/reports/Gender%20Wage%20Gap%20Final%20Report.pdf.

[10] 29 U.S.C. § 206(d)(1).

[11] Id.

[12] E.g. EEOC v. Madison Community United School District, 818 F.2d 577 (7th Cir. 1987)("equal work" requires a substantial identity rather than an absolute identity).

[13] 29 U.S.C. § 206(d)(1).

[14] 975 F.2d 1518 (11th Cir. 1992).

[15] 29 C.F.R. § 1620.27(a).

[16] 42 U.S.C. § 1981A. Compensatory damages include "future pecuniary losses, emotional pain, suffering, inconvenience, mental anguish, loss of enjoyment of life and other nonpecuniary losses." Punitive damages may be recovered where the employer acted "with malice or with reckless indifference" to the complaining employee's federally protected rights.

[17] The sum total of compensatory and punitive damages awarded may not exceed $50,000 in the case of an employer with more than 14 and fewer than 101 employees; $100,000 in the case of an employer with more than 100 and fewer than 201 employees; $200,000 in the case of an employer with more than 200 and fewer than 500 employees; and $300,000 in the case of an employer with more than 500 employees.

[18] 550 U.S. 618 (2007).

[19] 42 U.S.C. § 2000e-2(a)(1).

[20] Ledbetter v. Goodyear Tire & Rubber Co., 550 U.S. 618 (2007).

[21] P.L. 111-2.

[22] For more information on the Ledbetter decision and subsequent legislation, see CRS Report RS22686, Pay Discrimination Claims Under Title VII of the Civil Rights Act: A Legal Analysis of the Supreme Court's Decision in Ledbetter v. Goodyear Tire & Rubber Co., Inc., by Jody Feder.

[23] 222 F.R.D. 137 (N.D.Cal. 2004).

[24] Id. at 155.

[25] Id. at 142.

[26] Id. at 166.

[27] Dukes v. Wal-Mart, 509 F.3d 1168 (9th Cir. 2007).

[28] Dukes v. Wal-Mart Stores, Inc., 603 F.3d 571 (9th Cir. 2010).

[29] 131 S. Ct. 2541 (2011). The Court also unanimously held that claims for monetary relief may not be certified pursuant to Rule 23(b)(2), unless the monetary relief is incidental to the injunctive or declaratory relief. Id. at 2557.

[30] Fed. R. Civ. P. 23(a).

[31] Wal-Mart, 131 S. Ct. at 2554.

[32] Id. at 2553-56.

[33] Steve Painter, "Arkansas Democrat-Gazette," June 13, 2012.

[34] Ariel Barkhurst, "Women Sue Wal-Mart for Discrimination," Sun-Sentinel, October 5, 2012, p. 1D.

[35] Dukes v. Wal-Mart Stores, Inc., 2013 U.S. Dist. LEXIS 109106 (N.D. Cal. Aug. 2, 2013).

[36] Love v. Wal-Mart Stores, Inc., 2013 U.S. Dist. LEXIS 143234 (S.D. Fla. Sept. 23, 2013); Phipps v. Wal-Mart Stores, Inc., 925 F. Supp. 2d 875 (M.D. Tenn. 2013); Odle v. Wal-Mart Stores, Inc., 2012 U.S. Dist. LEXIS 159351 (N.D. Tex. Oct. 15, 2012).

[37] Dukes, 222 F.R.D. at 149.

[38] Brooke A. Masters, "Wall Street Sex-Bias Case Settled; Morgan Stanley Agrees to Pay $54 Million," Washington Post, July 13, 2004, at E01.

[39] Brooke A. Masters and Amy Joyce, "Costco is the Latest Class-Action Target; Lawyers' Interest Increases in Potentially Lucrative Discrimination Suits," Washington Post, August 18, 2004, at A01.

[40] 240 F.R.D. 627 (D. Cal. 2007).

[41] Ellis v. Costco Wholesale Corp., 657 F.3d 970 (9th Cir. Cal. 2011).

[42] Ellis v. Costco Wholesale Corp., 285 F.R.D. 492 (N.D. Cal. 2012).

[43] Id. at 509.

[44] 29 U.S.C. §§ 216-17.

[45] E.g. Hybki v. Alexander & Alexander, Inc., 536 F. Supp. 483 (W.D.Mo. 1982) (emphasizing damages for pain and suffering are not available under the EPA).

[46] See Fallon v. State of Illinois, 882 F.2d 1206 (7th Cir. 1989).

[47] During the 1980s, some litigants tried to substitute job equivalency for the "equal work standard" in the EPA through so-called "comparable worth" Title VII cases. Under the comparable worth principle, whole classes of jobs are undervalued because they traditionally have been predominately held by women. Because of alleged labor market bias against female-dominated jobs, Title VII plaintiffs contended that pay discrimination claims should not be limited by the EPA standard, requiring that jobs be substantially "equal" or similar for different pay rates to be considered discriminatory. Instead, Title VII wage-based discrimination actions against employers could be predicated on job evaluation studies, they argued, which compared the value of women's jobs to those of men who perform work that is dissimilar, but of equivalent or comparable worth to the employer. The courts, however, were not receptive to the comparable worth argument. See AFSCME v. State of Washington 770 F. 2d 1401 (9th Cir. 1985). See also, American Nurses Ass'n v. State of Illinois, 606 F. Supp. 1313 (N.D.Ill. 1985) (Congress never intended to incorporate a comparable worth standard in Title VII and such a concept is neither sound nor workable).

INDEX

D

E

F